Follow the
TRUE GOD
and Inherit Everlasting Life

GREGG GONZALES

INK START MEDIA
5710 W Gate City Blvd Ste K #284
Greensboro, NC 27407

The colors of this book represent the main colors of the Tabernacle; the portable earthly dwelling place of Yahweh that was used by the Israelites from the Exodus until the conquest of Canaan.

Blue represents Heaven and God's Divinity,

Purple represents Royalty,

Red represents Jesus' Blood.

FOLLOW THE TRUE GOD AND INHERIT EVERLASTING LIFE

Many Pastors and Evangelicals avoid controversial topics. Pastors and Evangelicals are responsible to bring to light all issues in the Bible, not just the ones that make us feel good. Some Pastors and Evangelicals use difficult words and descriptions to describe Biblical concepts; this book doesn't. Many people claim to be Christians and are fooling themselves. This book will help them to become True Christians, and Inherit Everlasting Life.

The whole idea of this book is to highlight the importance of being "Born Again" and receiving the "Holy Spirit", as mentioned in the New Covenant Jesus gave us.

This book is written in the way a freshman in high school can understand it, and is in big letters so seniors can view it more easily as well. The author's chapter on Boasting hasn't been written about, to the author's knowledge in any other books.

The following information is to help the reader to more easily understand how this book is arranged:

- Many people around the world claim to be Christians. However, many use the word loosely and without understanding its true meaning and value. Where possible, the author uses the word "True Christian".

- The word "Truth" means all the words in the Holy Bible and Truth is another name for Jesus Christ.

- Capitalizing and Underlining particular words and Scriptures are to show the significance of those words.

- Triune and Trinity mean the same. In this book, the author will use the word Triune.

- Most Bible Scriptures in this book are from the New International Version, for short, the NIV Bible.

- Scripture verses are always given with each topic. However, there are many more Scriptures for each topic that aren't quoted.

- Pictures are from the internet.

CHAPTER TITLES

Chapter 1 Can we Believe in the Bible? The Importance of the Bible. The "Truth" of the Bible. The consequences of adding and subtracting from the Bible. Manmade Rules show you don't Trust in God. Who is responsible for what is in the Bible? How to read the Bible? The Bible has many different names. Page 9

Chapter 2 The Attributes (Traits) of God. Some of the different names for God the Creator of all things. The Jewish and the Christian Festivals. The Triune (Trinity). The Old and New Testament Covenants. The difference between the Old Testament and the New Testament. Are the 10 Commandments in the New Testament? Page 17

Chapter 3 Is Jesus Worthy of Worship? Where are God and Jesus (physically) today? Who's going to Heaven? The Third Heaven, Paradise, and the Intermediate Heaven- they're all the same. Most True Christians will live on Earth. The Resurrected Jesus had a physical body. Christians to live on a new physical Earth. Heaven is described as a physical place. How is Hell described? Page 35

Chapter 4 Born Again as a New Creation. Page 43

Chapter 5 Who is the Holy Spirit? What is known about the Human Spirit and Soul that God gave us? Page 53

Chapter 6 False Religions that don't follow the True God. Page 61

Chapter 7 Boasting in the Bible. Page 111

Chapter 8 Various "True Christian" topics; The only Sacrifices a True Christians would participate in. How many years ago was Man created? Scriptures that say there's Life after death. Some things a True Christian would say or do. Do the Scriptures allow us to Judge? How Pastors should present themselves? Is Self-Defense and the Death Penalty allowed in the Bible? Page 117

Are Tithings (Contributions) mandatory? Why did God create us? How to Live and Relate to Others? Do we need to congregate with other True Christians? How can Believers be in the World, and not of the World? Health Benefits. Why is it so Important to Forgive others? How to defend the Truth (the Word of God in the Bible). Page 137

Chapter 9 Various Sinful topics; What does the Bible say about; Homosexuality, Transgenderism, Racism, Abortion, and Slavery? Astrology, Magic, Mediums, Wizards, Palm/Hand Readers, Tarot Card Readers and Sorcery. Evolution is the Biggest Lie in America. Page 157

CHAPTER 1

CAN WE BELIEVE IN THE BIBLE?

A. Archeology studies, for the last 150 years, have not come out with any evidence that deems any part of the Bible, whether it is historical or geographical, <u>not to be true</u>. In fact, many of the hundreds and thousands of excavations have supported the Bible.

B. The discovery of the Dead Sea Scrolls in 1947, in a cave on the western side of the Dead Sea, had over 800 pieces of the Old Testament and the whole book of Isaiah. When the pieces were put together, this discovery supported the accuracy of the Old Testament, with only minimal differences. Most of these books were from the first and second century B.C.

C. Currently there are over 24,000 manuscripts, portions, and versions of the New Testament that complement each other.

D. Approximately 27% of the entire Bible contains prophecies. There are 1,239 prophecies in the Old Testament, and 578 in the New Testament. Those prophecies that were supposed to have already taken place in time-have certainly happened.

E. There was over 540 people who witnessed the existence of Jesus Christ after His resurrection, and this happened on at least 10 different occasions.

F. Predating the Dead Sea Scrolls discovery is the findings of a Jewish burial, in 1979, that had two scrolls, called the 'Ketef Hinnom Scrolls' (in a cave), that dated to the late seventh century B.C. or early sixth century B.C. These scrolls contained the name Yahweh and priestly prayers from the book of Numbers. As of 2021, these scrolls are about 2,700 years old.

G. There have been many other discoveries, including villages, burials, and artifacts that support the Bible.

The Importance of the Bible

The first 5 books of the Bible (the Torah) are so holy to the Jews, that the Bible is treated as if it was a human. The Torah is never touched by the speaker. The Rabbi uses a finger made of wood or metal to read it. When the Torah becomes unreadable, it is buried in a human Jewish cemetery, just like a person.

The Bible is the top seller of all books in the world. As of 2020, the New Testament has been written in over 1,500 different languages. Sadly, many put it on their shelves or their coffee tables.

The Truth of the Bible

Hebrews 4:12 says, the Word of God is living and powerful, and in other Bibles it says, the Word of God is quick and powerful. The Greek word for quick means 'alive'.

2 Timothy 3:16-17 - All Scripture is God-breathed and is useful for teaching, rebuking, correcting, and training in righteousness, so that the servant of God may be thoroughly equipped for every good work.

1 Corinthians 15:1-4 - Now, brothers and sisters, I want to remind you of the gospel I preached to you, which you received and on which you have taken your stand. By this gospel, you are saved, if you hold firmly to the word I preached to you. Otherwise, you have believed in vain. For what I received, I passed on to you as of first importance, that Christ died

for our sins according to the Scriptures, that He was buried, that He was raised on the third day according to the Scriptures.

John 17:17 - Sanctify them by the truth; your word is truth.

John 8:31-32 - To the Jews who had believed Him, Jesus said, 'If you hold to my teaching, you are really my disciples. Then you will know the truth, and the truth will set you free.'

The Consequences of Adding and Subtracting from the Bible

The True Church, also called a Bible Church, will follow what God says in the Bible. Here's a good way to separate the True Church from false churches (religions).

Deuteronomy 4:2 - <u>You shall not add to the word</u> that I command you, nor take from it, that you may keep the commandments of the Lord your God that I command you.

Deuteronomy 12:32 - Everything that I command you, you shall be careful to do. <u>You shall not add to it or take from it.</u>

Revelation 22:18 - I warn everyone who hears the words of the prophecy of this book. **If anyone adds to them, God will add to him the plagues described in this book.**

Revelation 22:19 - And if anyone takes away from the words of the book of this prophecy, God will take away his share in the tree of life and in the holy city, which are described in this book.

Galatians 1:6-9 - I am astonished that you are so quickly deserting him, who called you in the grace of Christ, and are turning to a different gospel; not that there is another one, but there are some who trouble you and want to distort the gospel of Christ. But, **even if we or an angel from heaven should preach to you a gospel contrary to the one we preached to you, let him be accursed** [cursed, damned, doomed, condemned]. As we have said before, so now **I say again: If anyone is**

preaching to you a gospel contrary to the one you received, let him be accursed.

1 Corinthians 4:6 - **Now, brothers and sisters, I have applied these things to myself and Apollos for your benefit, so that you may learn from us the meaning of the saying, "Do not go beyond what is written." Then You will not be puffed up in being a follower of one of us over against the other.**

1 Thessalonians 4:8 - therefore, **he who rejects this instruction does not reject man, but God.**

Titus 2:1 - You must teach what is written in accordance with sound doctrine.

2 John 1:7 - Many deceivers, who do not acknowledge Jesus Christ as coming in the flesh, have gone out in the world. As it says in verse 10, if anyone comes to you and doesn't bring this teaching (of Jesus Christ), <u>do not take him into your house or welcome him.</u>

Man Made Rules shows you don't Trust in God

Mark 7:7 - These people honor me with their lips, but their hearts are far from me. They worship me in vain; their teachings are merely human rules.

Isaiah 29:13 - These people come near to me with their mouth and honor me with their lips, but their hearts are far from me. Their worship of me is made up only of rules taught by men.

Jesus to the Pharisees-Matthew 15:8-9: "You hypocrites! Isaiah was right when he prophesied about you: These people honor me with their lips, but their hearts are far from me. They worship me in vain; their teachings are merely human rules."

Colossians 2:8 - See to it that no one takes you captive through hollow and deceptive philosophy, <u>which depends on human tradition</u> and the elemental spiritual forces of this world, rather than on Christ.

Colossians 2:22-23 - These rules, which have to do with things that are all destined to perish with use, are based merely on human commands and teachings. Such regulations, indeed, have an appearance of wisdom, with their self-imposed worship, their false humility, and their harsh treatment of the body, but they lack any value in restraining sensual indulgence.

Psalms 118:8-9 - It is better to take refuge in the Lord than to trust in humans. It is better to take refuge in the Lord than to trust in princes.

Proverbs 3:5-6 - Trust in the Lord with all your heart, and lean not on your own understanding; in all your ways submit to Him, and He will make your paths straight.

Psalms 146:3 - Do not put your trust in princes, in human beings, who cannot save.

Isaiah 2:22 - Stop trusting in mere humans, who have but a breath in their nostrils. Why hold them in esteem?

Proverbs 30:5-6 - Every word of God is flawless; He is a shield to those who take refuge in Him. Do not add to His words, or He will rebuke you and prove you a liar.

Proverbs 28:26 - Those who trust in themselves are fools, but those who walk in wisdom are kept safe.

Acts 17:11 - Now, the Berean Jews were of more noble character than those in Thessalonica, for they received the message with great eagerness and examined the Scriptures every day to see if what Paul said was true.

Who is responsible for what is in the Bible

2 Peter 1:20 - Above all, you must understand that no prophecy of Scripture came about by the prophets own interpretation; for prophecy never had its origin in the will of man, but men spoke from God **as they were carried along by the Holy Spirit.**

2 Timothy 3:16 - All scripture is God-breathed and is useful for teaching, rebuking, correcting, and training in righteousness so that the man of God may be thoroughly equipped for every good work.

Galatians 1:11 - I want you to know, brothers and sisters, **that the gospel I preached is not of human origin**. I did not receive it from any man, nor was I taught it; rather, I received it by revelation from Jesus Christ.

How to Read the Bible

Most of the Bible, you read it word for word, as a matter of fact. Passages that say something like "You should cut off your right hand and toss it into the sea" are using figurative (fig-gry-uh tiv) words, and should not be taken literally. At times, the Bible author uses allegorical (al-le-gor-i-cal) stories, maybe using characters, events, or symbols to help get their point across or to help to understand difficult spiritual concepts. Most of the parables use allegorical words and so do some of the authors in various Books.

The Bible has many different names

The Word of the Lord, The Holy Scriptures, The Gospel, The Living Word, The Book of the Law, The Law of the Lord, The Word of God, The Message of Christ, The Good News, The Scroll, The Sword of the Spirit, The Scriptures, and the Truth. The word "Bible" is not in the original manuscripts.

In this book, the author will refer mostly to the Bible verses as the Scriptures and the Truth. Jesus is known as the "Truth".

The first two chapters of the Bible begin with the creation and the last two chapters of Revelation begin with the re-creation of the heavens and the earth.

Jesus' death on the cross is the most important event this world has ever seen. At the last moment of Jesus' life, He cried out on the cross, and inside the Temple in Jerusalem, the curtain between the Holy Place and the Most Holy Place (the immediate presence of the Almighty God) was torn from top to bottom. <u>Now</u>, we can communicate with God on our own. Hebrews 4:16 positively tells us "Let us then approach God's throne of grace with confidence…"

These two events- the curtain tearing and Jesus dying for our sins, opened up an opportunity for mankind to develop a personal relationship with the God who created us; <u>if we repent of our sins, follow Jesus, believe in the Truth, and get Born Again</u>, we can inherit Eternal Life, here in a New Earth with God and Jesus.

Why do we have sin and have to repent when Adam and Eve sinned, not us? We inherited this sin from them. Like your own parents, you inherit characteristics. Like machinery that makes toys, if there's an imperfection (defect) in the original toy, then all toys will have this imperfection.

CHAPTER 2

THE ATTRIBUTES (TRAITS) OF GOD

God is Spirit

John 4:24 tells us that God is Spirit.

Timothy 1:17 tells us that God is eternal, immortal (He will never die), and invisible. As a spirit, He can be in all places at the same time. He is not flesh and bone as the Mormons incorrectly depict Him.

Numbers 23:19 says that God is not human and that He doesn't lie.

John also tells us in 4:24, that his worshipers must worship in the Spirit and in Truth. The only way you can worship God is in Spirit, which means, you have to have the Holy Spirit in you. When you are Reborn you receive the Holy Spirit.

God Is Self-Existent

He has always existed. He has no beginning and no end. He exists independently of any other being. He alone was and is God. God is self-existent.

John 5:26 tells us God has life in Himself, and He gave his son life in himself. God is the Alpha and the Omega.

God Is Immutable

Immutable means that God does not change.

Malachi 3:6 tells us, "I, the Lord, do not change."

Psalms 102:25-27 says that God is the same and will endure forever.

Hebrews 6:17-18 tells us that it's impossible for God to Lie.

God is consistent with His written words in the Bible. For example, if an angel, human, or others came about, with new revelations that are different from the Bible, this would be totally false teachings.

God is Omnipotent

Omnipotent describes God as all-powerful. He has power over the wind, the sea, gravity, the sun, etc.

Revelation 1:4 - "...the ruler of all, who was and who is and who is to come..." Revelation 19:15 adds, "Coming out of his mouth is a sharp sword with which to strike down the nations. He will rule them with an iron scepter..."

God is Omnipresent

God's omnipresence means that God is everywhere. He has the ability to be anywhere and everywhere at the same time.

In Jeremiah 23:24, God says, "Do I not fill the heavens and the earth?"

God is Omniscient

The omniscience of God is the fact that God is all-knowing.

1 Chronicles 28:9 - "...the Lord searches every heart and understands every desire and every thought."

Psalm 147:4-5 states, "Great is our Lord and abundant in power; His understanding is beyond measure."

God is Transcendent

God is beyond the range of normal human experience.

Isaiah 40:12-15 - Who has measured the waters in the hollow of his hand, or with the breadth of his hand marked off the heavens? Who has held the dust of the earth in a basket, or weighed the mountains on the scales and the hills in a balance? Who can fathom [understand] the Spirit of the Lord, or instruct the Lord as his counselor?

Whom did the Lord consult to enlighten him, and who taught him the right way? Who was it that taught him knowledge, or showed him the path of understanding?

Surely the nations are like a drop in a bucket; they are regarded as dust on the scales; he weighs the islands as though they were fine dust.

God is not part of the creation. He is, in fact, the Creator who created everything apart from Himself. This is why the Eastern religion concept of pantheism is not true. This is also why the New Age and the Native Americans teaching of "Mother Earth" is not valid. God is not the earth or the cosmos. He is the Creator, not part of creation!

2 Chronicles 2:6 - But who is able to build a temple for him, since the heavens, even the highest heavens, cannot contain him? Who then am I to build a temple for him, except as a place to burn sacrifices before him?

He is not limited by our three-dimensional, naturalistic world, nor is He limited by the fourth dimension of time. God is supernatural, <u>beyond our natural understanding</u>.

Isaiah 55:9 - As the heavens are higher than the earth, so are my ways higher than your ways and my thoughts than your thoughts.

God is Sovereign

Isaiah 45:5-9 - I am the Lord, and there is no other; apart from me, there is no God. I will strengthen you, though you have not acknowledged me, so that from the rising of the sun to the place of its setting, people may know there is none besides me. I am the Lord, and there is no other. I form the light and create darkness.

I bring prosperity and create disaster; I, the Lord, do all these things. You heavens above rain down my righteousness; let the clouds shower it down. Let the earth open wide, let salvation spring up let righteousness flourish with it; I, the Lord, have created it. Woe to those who quarrel with their Maker, those who are nothing but potsherds among the potsherds on the ground. Does the clay say to the potter, 'What are you making?' Does your work say, 'The potter has no hands'?

Revelation 4:11 - You are worthy, our Lord and God, to receive glory and honor and power, for you created all things, and by your will, they were created and have their being.

God is Holy

Isaiah 6:3 - And they were calling to one another: "Holy, holy, holy is the Lord Almighty; the whole earth is full of his glory."

1 Samuel 2:2 - There is no one holy like the Lord; there is no one besides you; there is no rock like our God.

Psalm 99:9 - Exalt the Lord our God, and worship at his holy mountain, for the Lord our God is holy.

God is Truth

Psalm 100:5 - For the Lord is good and his love endures forever; his faithfulness continues through all generations.

Psalms 111:7 - The works of his hands are faithful and just; all his precepts are trustworthy.

Deuteronomy 32:4 - He is the Rock, his works are perfect, and all his ways are just. A faithful God who does no wrong, upright, and just is he.

God is Love

John 3:16 - <u>For God so loved the world that he gave his one and only Son</u>, that whoever believes in him shall not perish but have eternal life.

1 John 4:10 - This is love: not that we loved God, but that he loved us and sent his Son as an atoning sacrifice for our sins.

1 John 4:16 - And so we know and rely on the love God has for us. God is love. Whoever lives in love, lives in God, and God in them.

Some of the Different names for God the Creator of all things

1. El Eloah (El-Oh-ah): Mighty Power.

2. Elohim (Eloh-heem): God, Creator, Mighty and Strong.

3. El Shaddai (El-shah-dahy): Almighty, the Mighty One of Jacob.

4. Adonai ((Ah-daw-nahy): A sacred name to the Jews that is not uttered.

5. Lord; God used this name more with the Gentiles.

6. YHWH-Yahweh, with about 15 different variations.

7. LORD, all capitals, the proper name.

8. I AM who I AM; the name given to Moses.

9. Jealous; Showing His anger for idol worshiping.

Exodus 34:14 - Do not worship any other god, for the Lord, whose name is Jealous, is a jealous God.

Note: There are many more names for God. Jehovah is not one of them. Jehovah is an anglicized word for Yahweh, and Jehovah is not found in the manuscripts.

The Hebrews and Christian Festivals

The Hebrews were commanded by God to celebrate the following:

1. Passover

Leviticus 23:5 - The Lord's Passover begins at twilight on the fourteenth day of the first month.

Passover is in remembrance of the last plague in Egypt when the angel of death passed over the children of Israel.

2. The Feast of Unleavened Bread

Leviticus 23:6 - The Lord's Passover begins at twilight on the fourteenth day of the first month.

This feast follows the start of Passover. In the rush of leaving Egypt, there was no time to add leaven (yeast) to their bread. The Jews don't use yeast in the bread during this celebration, and remember the ancestor's hard life in Egypt. Otherwise, Jewish Rabbi authorities allow the use of chemical leavening such as baking powder.

3. Feast of the First Fruits

Leviticus 23:10 - Speak to the Israelites and say to them: "When you enter the land I am going to give you and you reap its harvest, bring to the priest a sheaf of the first grain you harvest."

This is a harvest festival thanking God for all that He provides.

4. Feast of Weeks or Pentecost

Leviticus 23:16 - Count off fifty days up to the day after the seventh Sabbath, and then present an offering of new grain to the Lord.

The feast is a harvest feast and the remembrance of when God gave them the Ten Commandments.

5. Feast of Trumpets

Leviticus 23:23-25 - The Lord said to Moses, "Say to the Israelites: 'On the first day of the seventh month you are to have a day of Sabbath rest, a sacred assembly commemorated with trumpet blasts. Do no regular work, but present a food offering to the Lord.'"

This is a rest time for Jews, with a food offering to God.

6. Day of Atonement

Leviticus 16:8-34 - He is to cast lots for the two goats, one lot for the Lord and the other for the scapegoat. Aaron shall bring the goat whose lot falls to the Lord, and sacrifice it as a sin offering. But the goat chosen by the lot as the scapegoat shall be presented alive before the Lord to be used for making atonement, by sending it into the wilderness as a scapegoat.

This is a day of atonement, a day of repentance, and a time to get right with God.

7. Feast of the Tabernacles or Booths

Leviticus 23:34-36 - Say to the Israelites: 'On the fifteenth day of the seventh month the Lord's Festival of Tabernacles begins, and it lasts for seven days. [35] The first day is a sacred assembly; do no regular work. For seven days present food offerings to the LORD and on the eighth day hold a sacred assembly and present a food offering to the Lord. It is the closing special assembly; do no regular work.

Celebrating God's protection and provisions for the 40 years their ancestors spent in the wilderness.

Luke 22:7-19 – Then came the day of Unleavened Bread on which the Passover lamb had to be sacrificed. Jesus sent Peter and John, saying, "Go and make preparations for us to eat the Passover."

"Where do you want us to prepare for it?" they asked.

He replied, "As you enter the city, a man carrying a jar of water will meet you. Follow him to the house that he enters, [11] and say to the owner of the house, 'The Teacher asks: Where is the guest room, where I may eat the Passover with my disciples?' He will show you a large room upstairs, all furnished. Make preparations there." They left and found things just as Jesus had told them. So they prepared the Passover.

When the hour came, Jesus and his apostles reclined at the table. And he said to them, "I have eagerly desired to eat this Passover with you before I suffer. For I tell you, I will not eat it again until it finds fulfillment in the kingdom of God."

After taking the cup, he gave thanks and said, "Take this and divide it amongst yourselves. For I tell you, I will not drink again from the fruit of the vine until the kingdom of God comes." And he took the bread, gave thanks and broke it, and gave it to them, saying,

"This is my body given for you; do this in remembrance of me."

The Lord's Evening Meal is also called the Memorial and the Last Supper.

The Jewish celebrations were done away with, by Jesus' sacrifice for us. So, the only celebration we should partake in is the Memorial/Last Supper that Jesus commanded us to participate in.

From the above, we see that God and Jesus were the ones who decided what celebrations we should honor.

With the man-made celebrations in the Catholic Church, pagan holidays were reclassified as Christian holy days (probably to attract the Roman pagans).

The Roman Lupercalia; an ancient pagan bloody sexual pagan festival, held each year on February the 15th, took the place of Valentines (according to some historians). After sacrificing a goat and a dog, the people would have a celebration of fertility rites and romance.

The pagan feast of the purification of Isis is a yearly pagan celebration in honor of the goddess Isis; held on March the 5th, and replaced by the Feast of the Nativity (celebrating the birth of Mary).

Easter comes from the name Eostre - the pagan goddess of spring. Easter eggs and Easter bunnies are associated with Eostre, the symbol of rebirth and fertility. This celebration was held around March 15th and dedicated to the goddess Anna Perenna.

Halloween came from the pagan festival of Samhain which was dedicated to the memory of the dead and held on November the 2nd. Pope Boniface in the 5th century moved the celebration to May; however, the fire festival of October and November continued. In the 9th century, Pope Gregory moved the celebration back to the time of the fire festivals and called it All Saints Day.

Saturnalia was held annually from December the 17th through the 23rd. All work was halted during the celebration, even for the slaves. People decorated their homes with wreaths and other greenery. This celebration consisted of singing, gambling, feasting, giving others gifts, and a sacrifice at the temple of Saturn. The Christmas holiday owes many of its traditions to the Roman festival of Saturnalia. The first Catholic Christmas was in 336 A.D.

These manmade holidays (with roots in pagan worship) have caused financial burdens on many with the buying of gifts, hosting parties, and purchasing costumes/supplies. People who suffer from emotional problems generally get worse during the holidays, some even commit suicide. People generally drink more alcoholic beverages and eat more during these celebrations. Many people claim that stress increases during these times. <u>In the Bible, neither God nor Jesus required, asked for, or commanded these celebrations.</u>

Jesus' approximate birth, ministry and death

Luke 2:8-11 - And there were shepherds living out in the fields nearby, keeping watch over their flocks at night. An angel of the Lord appeared to them, and the glory of the Lord shone around them, and they were terrified. But the angel said to them, "Do not be afraid. I bring you good news that will cause great joy for all the people. Today in the town of David a Savior has been born to you; he is the Messiah, the Lord."

The shepherds in Jerusalem would not stay in the fields in the month of December, it was too cold.

In Luke 2:1-4, Joseph and Mary came to Bethlehem to register for the census. The Roman government wouldn't have had people traveling to register in the cold.

In Luke 1:26, Elizabeth, while in her six-month pregnancy, God sent the angel Gabriel to visit Mary and told her that she would conceive a Son and name him Jesus. That would mean Jesus was six months younger than John the Baptist. Jesus was probably born in late September or October.

Jesus was baptized in about 27 A.D. Since most prophets began their ministry at 30 years old, Jesus was born in about 3 B.C. In about 31 A.D. Jesus was crucified, thus putting an end to sacrificing animals and the priesthood forever.

The Triune (Trinity)

Triune (Trinity) is the union of three persons, The Father, The Son, and The Holy Spirit. Or, we can say the union of three divine persons; The Father, The Son, and The Holy Spirit. All three can be completely separate and all three can be united.

Below, we see the best example of the Triune, concerning God and Jesus. In these first two Scriptures, "The Lord" is God, himself, speaking. In the second scripture, God is telling us what is going to happen to Him. But, what actually happened was the death of Jesus as a human being.

Zechariah 12:1 - <u>The Lord</u>, who stretches out the heavens, who lays the foundation of the earth, and who forms the human spirit within a person, <u>declares</u>:

Zechariah 12:10 - And I will pour out on the house of David and the inhabitants of Jerusalem a spirit of grace and supplication. <u>They will look on me, the one they have pierced</u>, and they will mourn for him as one mourns for an only child, and grieve bitterly for him [Jesus] as one grieves for a firstborn son

In the two Scriptures below, how did the Apostle John know that the Word, another name for Jesus, was with God and is God? The Apostle John was not around in the beginning or during the creations of all things. John knew because he was under the inspiration of, or under the influence of the Holy Spirit. In other words, the Holy Spirit is really the author of the book of John and all of the books of the Bible.

John 1:1 - In the beginning, was the Word, and the Word was with God, and the <u>Word was God.</u>

John 8:58 "Very truly I tell you," Jesus answered, "before Abraham was born, <u>I am</u>!" The name "I Am" is another name for God

More Scriptures on the Triune:

Col 1:16-17 - <u>In him [Jesus] all things were created</u>: things in heaven and on earth, visible and invisible, whether thrones or powers or rulers or authorities; all things have been created through him and for him. <u>He is before all things, and in him, all things hold together</u>

Titus 2:13 - While we wait for the blessed hope—<u>the appearing of the glory of our great God and Savior, Jesus Christ</u>

Hebrews 1:3 - The Son is the radiance of God's glory, <u>and the exact representation of his being</u>, sustaining all things by his powerful word. After he had provided purification for sins, he sat down at the right hand of the Majesty in heaven.

Acts 5:1-4 - Now a man named Ananias, together with his wife Sapphira, also sold a piece of property. With his wife's full knowledge he kept back part of the money for himself, but brought the rest and put it at the apostles' feet. ³Then Peter said, "Ananias, how is it that Satan has so filled your heart that you have lied to the Holy Spirit and have kept for yourself some of the money you received for the land? ⁴ Didn't it belong to you before it was sold? And after it was sold, wasn't the money at your disposal? What made you think of doing such a thing? <u>You have not lied just to human beings but to God.</u>

Genesis 1:2 - Now the earth was formless and empty, darkness was over the surface of the deep, and the [Holy] Spirit of God was hovering over the waters.

John 14:15-18 - If you love me, keep my commands. ¹⁶ And I will ask the Father, and he will give you another advocate to help you and be with you forever— ¹⁷ the Spirit of truth. The world cannot accept him, because it neither sees him nor knows him. But you know him, for he lives with you and will be in you. ¹⁸ I will not leave you as orphans; I will come to you.

Acts 4:31 - After they prayed, the place where they were meeting was shaken. And they were all filled with the Holy Spirit and spoke the word of God boldly.

The Old and New Testament Covenants

The Old Covenant was given to the Hebrews by Moses
and was a foreshadow of the New Covenant.

Note: God's chosen people were first called Hebrews, up until their conquest of Canaan (Palestine); which happened in about 1250 B.C., thereafter they were referred to as the Israelites. After the Israelites returned from Babylonian Exile in 538 B.C., they became known as the Jews.

- God promised the Hebrew people that they would be His chosen people and He would be their God

Deuteronomy 7:6-8 - For you are a people holy to the Lord your God. The Lord your God has chosen you, out of all the peoples on the face of the earth, to be his people, his treasured possession.

- The Ten Commandments would be the foundation of what God expected of the people; altogether there were 613 laws.

- God promised to create a mighty nation for the Hebrews with many descendants.

Genesis 12:2 - <u>I will make you into a great nation</u>, and I will bless you; I will make your name great, and you will be a blessing.

Genesis 15:5 - He took him outside and said, "Look up at the sky and count the stars—if indeed you can count them." Then he said to him, "So shall your offspring be."

Also Genesis 17:2-7 and 35:11.

- To give them a promised land.

Genesis 13:15 - All the land that you see I will give to you and your offspring forever.

Genesis 15:18-21 - On that day the Lord made a covenant with Abram and said, "To your descendants, I give this land, from the Wadi of Egypt to the great river, the Euphrates."

Genesis 17:7-8 - I will establish my covenant as an everlasting covenant.

- And make them great among the other nations.

Genesis 22:17 - I will surely bless you and make your descendants as numerous as the stars in the sky and as the sand on the seashore. Your descendants will take possession of the cities of their enemies.

Genesis 27:28-29 - May nations serve you.

28:13-14 - I will give you and your descendants the land.

- Protection from their enemies and good health.

Deuteronomy 7:15 - The Lord will keep you free from every disease. He will not inflict on you the horrible diseases you knew in Egypt, but he will inflict them on all who hate you.

Numbers 14:9 - Only do not rebel against the Lord. And do not be afraid of the people of the land, because we will devour them. Their protection is gone, but the Lord is with us. Do not be afraid of them.

- Faithfulness to God brings blessings.

Deuteronomy 11:13 – So, if you faithfully obey the commands I am giving you today, to love the Lord your God and to serve him with all your heart and with all your soul, 14 then I will send rain on your land in its season, both autumn and spring rains, so that you may gather in your grain, new wine, and olive oil. 15 I will provide grass in the fields for your cattle, and you will eat and be satisfied.

- Animal sacrifice would compensate for their sins which provided a system where the Hebrews could maintain a good relationship with God when they sinned.

Leviticus 5:10 - The priest shall then offer the other as a burnt offering in the prescribed way and make atonement for them for the sin they have committed, and they will be forgiven.

- Males had to be circumcised.

Genesis 17:10-14 - Every male among you shall be circumcised, every male among you who is 8 days old.

- The Sabbath had to be observed.

- The Hebrews had to obey rules for dietary, social, and hygiene.

In the book of Leviticus, all of chapter 11 covers the different animals they could and could not eat.

Leviticus 15:4-27 - Covers bathing and washing clothes when a woman has a discharge of blood.

The Old Testament covenant had many High Priests; the ark was a sign of salvation, Moses and Prophets were mediators between God and the people, the covenant needed yearly offerings for sin and the covenant was just for the Hebrews.

The New Testament Covenant given by Jesus replaced the Old Testament Covenant;

- The New Testament is for all men and women, not just the Hebrews.

- Total Forgiveness of sins if you're Born Again.

- Everlasting life.

- Jesus as our Mediator and Intercessor.

- The gift of the Holy Spirit for those that are Born Again.

The New Covenant is based on repentance, believing in Jesus and the Bible, and becoming Born Again.

Note: There was a total of 7 Covenants that God established with men in the Bible; first with Noah, Abraham, Moses, Aaron, Israel, David, and the New Covenant by Jesus Christ to all mankind.

Differences between the Old Testament and the New Testament;

- The Old Testament foreshadows Jesus and the New Testament reveals him.

- The Old Testament focused on the Laws and the New Testament was the fulfillment of the Law.

- Some of the Old Testament prophecies were about the coming of Jesus and the New Testament fulfilled his First Coming and speaks of his Second Coming.

- The Old Testament shows God's constant efforts to get the Hebrews to follow, the New Testament shows His offer of grace to all mankind.

Are the 10 Commandments in the New Testament?

Note: OT stands for Old Testament and NT stands for New Testament:

The Ten Commandments can be found in Exodus 20:2-17 and Deuteronomy 5:6-21.

OT- **Don't have other gods**

NT- *Matthew 4:10 ... 'Worship the Lord your God, and serve him only.'*

OT- **Do not make idols or images**

NT- *1 John 5:21 - Dear children, keep yourselves from idols.*

OT- **Do not take the name of the Lord in vain**

NT- *1 Timothy 6:1 - All who are under the yoke of slavery should consider their masters worthy of full respect, so that God's name and our teaching may not be slandered.*

(Vain means- for wicked, worthless, and wrong purposes).

OT- **Remember the Sabbath**

NT- *Acts 13:42 - As Paul and Barnabas were leaving the synagogue, the people invited them to speak further about these things on the next Sabbath.*

OT- **Honor your father and mother**

NT- *Ephesians 6:1 - Children, obey your parents.*

OT- **Do not kill**

NT- Matthew 19:18 - …Jesus replied,

You shall not murder,

You shall not commit adultery,

You shall not steal,

You shall not give false testimony

NT- Romans 13:9 - The commandments, "You shall not commit adultery," "You shall not murder," "You shall not steal," "You shall not covet," and whatever other command there may be, are summed up in this one command: "Love your neighbor as yourself"

OT- **Do not commit adultery**

NT- Galatians 5:19-21 - The acts of the flesh are obvious: sexual immorality, impurity, and debauchery; [20] idolatry and witchcraft; hatred, discord, jealousy, fits of rage, selfish ambition, dissensions, factions [21] and envy; drunkenness, orgies, and the like. I warn you, as I did before, that those who live like this will not inherit the kingdom of God.

NT- Matthew 19:18 Jesus replied, "You shall not murder, you shall not commit adultery, you shall not steal, you shall not give false testimony."

OT- **Do not steal**

NT- Ephesians 4:28 - Anyone who has been stealing must steal no longer, but must work, doing something useful with their own hands, that they may have something to share with those in need.

OT- **Do not bear false witnesses** *(don't lie, don't deceive others)*

NT- Matthew 19:18 Jesus replied, "You shall not murder, you shall not commit adultery, you shall not steal, you shall not give false testimony."

OT- **Do not covet** (*to wrongfully desire what's not yours and to be resentful to those who have it*).

NT- *Romans 7:7* - What shall we say, then? Is the law sinful? Certainly not! Nevertheless, I would not have known what sin was, had it not been for the law. For I would not have known what coveting really was if the law had not said, "You shall not covet."

NT- *Romans 13:9* The commandments, "You shall not commit adultery," "You shall not murder," "You shall not steal," "You shall not covet," and whatever other command there may be, are summed up in this one command: "Love your neighbor as yourself.

Emperor Constantine

In AD 321, the Roman Emperor Constantine formally adopted the seven-day week and made Sunday the Christian Sabbath. In AD 364, the Catholic Council of Laodicea (La-o-de-cia) said, "Christians must not Judaize by resting on the Sabbath, but must work on that day, rather honoring the Lord's Day" (Sunday). Sunday is the day Jesus rose from the dead, or we could say the day of his resurrection. The changing of the Sabbath to Sunday by the Catholic Council was not surprising, because Christians had been celebrating the Sabbath on Sundays for hundreds of years before this ruling.

The Sabbath was changed to Sunday by the pagan emperor. We should be honoring the Sabbath from Friday evening at sunset to Saturday evening at sunset-Genesis 2:3 and Exodus 20:11.

CHAPTER 3

Note: much of the heading essences come from the superb book "Heaven" by Randy Alcorn.

Is Jesus worthy of Worship?

-Hebrews 1:6 - When God brings his firstborn into the world, he says, "Let all God's <u>angels worship him</u>."

-Daniel 7:13-14 - In my vision at night, I looked, and there before me was one like a son of man, coming with the clouds of heaven. He approached the Ancient of Days and was led into his presence. He was given authority, glory, and sovereign power; all nations <u>and peoples of every language worshiped him</u>. His dominion is an everlasting dominion that will not pass away, and his kingdom is one that will never be destroyed.

-Matthew 14:32-33 - And when they climbed into the boat, the wind died down. Then those who were in the boat <u>worshiped him</u>, saying, "Truly you are the Son of God."

-John 9:38 - Then the man said, "Lord, I believe," and he <u>worshiped him</u> (a blind man talking to Jesus).

This next section will clearly show that God and Jesus are physically in Heaven until the Second Coming of Jesus Christ. Some religions, like the Catholic Church, claim that Jesus is physically in the Eucharist, and as we see below and in later chapters, this is completely false.

Where are God and Jesus (physically) today?

- Psalm 115:3 - Our God is in heaven.

- Ecclesiastics 5:2 - God is in Heaven and you are on earth.

- Acts 3:21 - Heaven must receive him [Jesus] until the time comes for God to restore everything.

- Acts 7:55 - Stephen, filled with the Holy Spirit looked up to heaven and saw the glory of God and Jesus standing at the right hand of God.

- Ephesians 1:20 - …when he [God] raised him from the dead and seated him at his right hand in the heavenly realms, far above all rule and authority…

- Colossians 3:1 - Christ is seated at the right hand of God

- Hebrews 8:1 - we do have a high priest, who sat down at the right hand of the throne of the majesty in heaven.

- Revelation 22:7 - Behold, I am coming soon

(Meaning Jesus is not physically present on earth).

Who's going to Heaven?

Heaven was made for the angels and other angelic beings, with a few exceptions like the 144,000, poor in spirit, the persecuted, and the apostles. God's whole intent was to make earth for human beings (that's where Adam and Eve lived). After the 1000 year reign of Jesus Christ on Earth, that is where most of those who are Saved will live.

Many preachers talk about those who were saved and died, and now are in heaven. Actually, the souls of those who are saved go to the third heaven, which is also called paradise or the intermediate heaven.

- John 3:13 - No one has ever gone to Heaven.

- John 14:2 - I'm going to prepare a place for you (Jesus speaking to the Apostles).

Many preachers will say that this Scripture applies to everyone who is saved. But when reading Scripture, you want to pay attention to-who is speaking, what is their authority, and to whom they are speaking to. Jesus was speaking to the apostles only.

- Matthew 5:3 - the poor in spirit, for theirs is the kingdom of Heaven. -5:10 - Blessed are those who are persecuted because of righteousness, for theirs is the kingdom of heaven.

- Revelation 14:1-3 - Then I looked, and there before me was the Lamb, standing on Mount Zion, and with him, 144,000 who had his name and his Father's name written on their foreheads. [2] And I heard a sound from heaven like the roar of rushing waters and like a loud peal of thunder. The sound I heard was like that of harpists playing their harps. [3] And they sang a new song before the throne, and before the four living creatures and the elders. No one could learn the song except the 144,000 who had been redeemed from the earth.

Two well-known prophets that are not in Heaven;

- Acts 2:34 - David did not ascend into Heaven.

- Daniel 12:13 - Daniel will rest and then at the end of the days will rise to receive his allotted inheritance.

The Third Heaven-Paradise and the Intermediate Heaven there are all the same

-Luke 23:43 - Jesus answered him, "I tell you the truth, today you will be with me in paradise (Jesus speaking to the person hanging on a cross next to Him)."

-2 Corinthians 12:2 - Paul the Apostle is speaking and said, "I know a man in Christ who 14 years ago was caught up to <u>the third heaven,</u>12:4 was <u>caught up to paradise.</u>

Most True Christians will live on Earth

Revelation 21:1-2, "And I saw the holy city, New Jerusalem, coming down out of heaven from God."

Revelation 21:3-4 - <u>He will live with them, and they shall be his people, and God himself will be with them;</u> he will wipe away every tear from their eyes, and death shall be no more, neither shall there be mourning nor crying nor pain anymore, for the former things have passed away.

Revelation 22:1-5 - Then the angel showed me the river of the water of life, as clear as crystal, flowing from the throne of God and of the Lamb down the middle of the great street of the city [Jerusalem]. On each side of the river, stood the tree of life, bearing twelve crops of fruit, yielding its fruit every month. And the leaves of the tree are for the healing of the nations. No longer will there be any curse. <u>The throne of God and the Lamb will be in the city, and his servants will serve him.</u> They will see his face, and his name will be on their foreheads. <u>There will be no more night. They will not need the light of a lamp or the light of the sun, for the Lord God will give them light</u>. And they will reign forever and ever.

2 Peter 3:13 - In keeping with his promise, we are looking forward to a new heaven and a new earth.

Why would people want to go to heaven if God and Jesus are going to live on earth?

The Resurrected Jesus had a physical body

- Luke 24:39 - <u>Look at my hands and my feet</u>. It is I myself! Touch me and see; a ghost does not have flesh and bones, as you see I have."

- John 20:15-16 - He asked her, "Woman, why are you crying? Who is it you are looking for?" <u>Thinking he was the gardener</u>, she said, "Sir, if you have carried him away, tell me where you have put him, and I will get him." [16] Jesus said to her, "Mary." <u>She turned toward him</u> and cried out in Aramaic, "Rabboni!" (Which means "Teacher").

- Acts 1:11 - Men of Galilee, they said, Why do you stand here looking into the sky? This same Jesus, who has been taken from you into heaven, <u>will come back in the same way you have seen him go into heaven.</u>

Christians to live on a New physical Earth

We were created from the dust of the earth, and like God's original intentions with Adam and Eve; the majority of those Saved will live on a New Earth.

Revelation 21:1-3 - Then I saw "A new heaven and a new earth," for the first heaven and the first earth had passed away, and there was no longer any sea.

[2] I saw the Holy City, the New Jerusalem, coming down out of heaven from God, prepared as a bride beautifully dressed for her husband. [3] And I heard a loud voice from the throne saying, "Look! God's dwelling place is now among the people," and he will dwell with them. They will be his people, and God himself will be with them and be their God.

Revelation 22:1 - Then the angel showed me the river of the water of life, as clear as crystal, flowing from the throne of God and of the Lamb.

Ecclesiastics 1:4 - Generations come and generations go, but the earth remains forever.

Luke 22:29-30 - And I confer on you a kingdom, just as my Father conferred one on me, so that you may eat and drink at my table in my kingdom and sit on thrones, judging the twelve tribes of Israel.

Heaven is described as a physical place

Acts 7:55-56 - But Stephen, full of the Holy Spirit, <u>looked up to heaven and saw the glory of God, and Jesus standing at the right hand of God.</u> [56] "Look," he said, "I see heaven open and the Son of Man standing at the right hand of God.

Revelation 15-8 - And <u>the temple was filled with smoke</u> from the glory of God and from his power, and no one could enter the temple until the seven plagues of the seven angels were completed.

Revelation 8:6 - Then, <u>the seven angels who had the seven trumpets prepared to sound them.</u>

Revelation 19:14 - The armies of heaven <u>were following him, riding on white horses and dressed in fine linen, white and clean.</u>

Revelation 19:9 - Elijah, Luke, John, Isaiah, and Ezekiel <u>wrote about what they saw in heaven.</u>

Hebrews 8:5 - <u>They serve at a sanctuary that is a copy and shadow of what is in heaven</u>. This is why Moses was warned when he was about to build the tabernacle: "See to it that you make everything according to the pattern shown you on the mountain."

How is Hell described?

It will be beyond anything you could imagine.

Matthew 13:50 describes a blazing furnace, weeping and gnashing of teeth, Matthew 25:30 weeping and gnashing of teeth, Matthew 8:12 darkness, Luke 16:24 agony, Luke 16:23 torment, Matthew 25:46 eternal punishment.

-Jesus talked more about hell than any other Bible author, and he talked about hell more than heaven.

Matthew 10:28 - Do not be afraid of those who kill the body but cannot kill the soul. Rather, be afraid of the One who can destroy both soul and body in hell.

Matthew 13:40-42 states-As the weeds are pulled up and burned in the fire, so it will be at the end of the age. [41] The Son of Man will send out his angels, and they will weed out of his kingdom everything that causes sin and all who do evil. [42] They will throw them into the blazing furnace, where there will be weeping and gnashing of teeth.

The lake of fire will become the permanent Hell

Revelation 20:14-15 - Then death and Hades were thrown into the lake of fire. The lake of fire is the second death. [15] Anyone whose name was not found written in the book of life was thrown into the lake of fire.

CHAPTER 4

BORN AGAIN AS A NEW CREATION

Propitiation is the act of satisfying and obtaining favor from God and avoiding Godly punishment. With a Holy and Righteous God, all sins have to be dealt with. Because of man's sin, a <u>pure</u>, <u>perfect,</u> and <u>sinless</u> offering had to be sacrificed. Jesus offered to be this sacrifice. So, Jesus obtained favor from God for us.

Reparation is the reversing, repairing, or correcting for a wrong one has done. So, **atonement** is making it right. Other words for atonement are penance, redemption, reparation, amends, expiation, indemnification, payment, and propitiation.

Righteousness is the quality or state of being morally correct and justifiable. No person is righteous in God's eye.

Isaiah 64:6 - All of us have become like one who is unclean, and all our righteous acts are like filthy rags; we all shrivel up like a leaf, and like the wind, our sins sweep us away.

Romans 3:10 - As it is written: "There is no one righteous, not even one."

However, one can become righteous with God. 1 John 3:7- "The one who does what is right is righteous…"

According to Titus 3:3-7; at one time we too were foolish, disobedient, deceived and enslaved by all kinds of passions and pleasures. We lived in malice and envy, being hated and hating one another. But when the kindness and love of God our Savior appeared, he saved us, not because of righteous things we had done, but because of his mercy. He saved us through the washing of rebirth and renewal by the Holy Spirit, whom he poured out on us generously through Jesus Christ our Savior, [7] so that, having been justified by his grace, we might become heirs having the hope of eternal life.

Born Again, Reborn, or becoming A New Creation is a person who has repented, accepted Jesus as his Savior, and has made a commitment to follow Him.

Ephesians 2:8-9 tells us, "For it is by grace you have been saved, through faith, and this is not from yourselves, it is the gift of God-not by [your] works so that no one can boast." Once you were a slave of sin **and now you're a slave of Righteousness**. From this point on, you hate sin and love Righteousness.

By grace, you have experienced a spiritual rebirth, not a physical rebirth. With this rebirth, the Holy Spirit comes and lives inside you. The Holy Spirit gives that person the power to follow Jesus and become a witness for Him. The Holy Spirit convicts us of our sins, and by repentance we develop godly qualities and inherit spiritual gifts, to help fulfill our mission for Jesus Christ.

Justification is the act of God, in moving a willing person from the state of sin to the state of grace (justification).

Regeneration is the work of the Holy Spirit in changing that person from spiritual death to spiritual life.

Sanctification is a process by the Holy Spirit of changing a Born Again person's whole behavior. Sanctification is a continuous growth process for the rest of that person's life.

Salvation, Deliverance, or Redemption is the saving of a person from spiritual death and separation from God.

Here's the Steps to being Reborn/Born Again/becoming A New Creation (all share the same meaning).

Repentance is our first step in getting right with God

We need to tell God and others about our sins. However, only God can forgive sins. 1 John 1:9 says, "If we confess our sins, He [God] is faithful and just and will forgive us our sins and purify us from all unrighteousness".

James 5:16 states, "Therefore, confess your sins to one another and pray for one another, that you may be healed."

The Greek definition of repentance is to change one's way of life as the result of a complete change of thought and attitude with regard to sin and righteousness. This means you don't go back to doing the same sin over and over. You, with the help of God, change your ways. You need God's help, because on your own and being born with sin, you'll fail.

Repentance is the act of leaving what God has prohibited and following or returning to what he has commanded.

2 Corinthians 7:10 - Godly sorrow brings repentance that leads to salvation and leaves no regret, but worldly sorrow brings death.

The king of Nineveh issued a decree;

Jonah 3:8-10 – "But let people and animals be covered with sackcloth. Let everyone call urgently on God. Let them give up their evil ways and their violence. ⁹ Who knows? God may yet relent and with compassion turn from his fierce anger so that we will not perish."

¹⁰ When God saw what they did and how they turned from their evil ways, he relented and did not bring on them the destruction he had threatened.

Mark 1:15 – "The time has come," he said. "The kingdom of God has come near. Repent and believe the good news!"

Luke 5:32 - I have not come to call the righteous, but sinners to repentance.

With repentance comes forgiveness

1 John 1:9- If we confess our sins, he is faithful and just and will forgive us our sins and <u>purify us from all unrighteousness.</u>

2 Chronicles 7:14 - if my people, who are called by my name, will humble themselves and pray and seek my face and turn from their wicked ways, then I will hear from heaven, and I will forgive their sin and will heal their land.

2 Timothy 2:25-26 - Opponents must be gently instructed, in the hope that God will grant them repentance leading them to a knowledge of the truth, and that they will come to their senses and escape from the trap of the devil, who has taken them captive to do his will.

Mark 1:15 - "Repent and believe in the gospel."

Acts 17:30 - "He commands all people everywhere to repent."

Our Second step is to follow the Truth and accept Jesus Christ as our Savior.

In John 14:6 Jesus said, "I am the way, the truth, and the life."

If were following Jesus, we are following the Truth that is in the Bible.

More Scriptures on Truth:

John 8:32 - Then you will know the truth, and the truth will set you free.

Psalms 119:160 - All your words are true; all your righteous laws are eternal.

John 1:14 - The Word became flesh and made his dwelling among us. We have seen his glory, the glory of the one and only Son, who came from the Father, <u>full of grace and truth.</u>

1 John 5:12 - <u>He who has the Son has life</u>; he who does not have the Son of God does not have life.

John 3:18 - <u>Whoever believes in him is not condemned, but whoever does not believe, stands condemned already</u>, because he has not believed in the name of God's one and only Son.

Psalms 25:4-5 - Show me your ways, Lord, teach me your paths. <u>Guide me in your truth</u> and teach me, for you are God my Savior, and my hope is in you all day long.

Romans 1:25 - They exchanged the truth about God for a lie and worshiped and served created things rather than the Creator—who is forever praised. Amen.

Titus 1:1 - Paul, a servant of God and an apostle of Jesus Christ to further the faith of God's elect and their knowledge of the truth that leads to godliness

The Bible is very clear that there is one and only one way to God's kingdom, and that is through Jesus Christ. <u>All religions that say otherwise are false religions.</u>

John 14:6 - I am the way and the truth and the life. <u>No one comes to the Father except through me</u>.

John 3:36 - Whoever believes in the Son has eternal life, <u>but whoever rejects the Son will not see life</u>, for God's wrath remains on him.

Acts 4:12 - Peter said, <u>salvation is found in no one else</u>, for there is no other name under heaven given to men, by which we must be saved.

Why does a person need to be Born Again?

About four years ago, I asked this question to GotQuestions.org, which is one of the best sources concerning the Bible.

Question:
As mentioned in your book; explain how one can be reborn, and why only those who are reborn, have their sins forgiven and have a relationship with God?

Answer:
The classic passage from the Bible that answers this question is John 3:1-21. The Lord Jesus Christ is talking to Nicodemus, a prominent Pharisee,

and member of the Sanhedrin (the ruling body of the Jews). Nicodemus had come to Jesus at night with some questions.

As Jesus talked with Nicodemus, He said, "I tell you the truth, no one can see the kingdom of God unless he is born again. How can a man be born when he is old?" Nicodemus asked, "Surely he cannot enter a second time into his mother's womb to be born". Jesus answered, "I tell you the truth, no one can enter the kingdom of God unless he is born of water and the Spirit. Flesh gives birth to flesh, but the Spirit gives birth to spirit. You should not be surprised at my saying, You must be born again" (John 3:3-7).

The phrase "born again" literally means "born from above." Nicodemus had a real need. He needed a change of his heart; a spiritual transformation. New birth, being born again, is an act of God whereby eternal life is imparted to the person who believes (2 Corinthians 5:17, Titus 3:5, 1 Peter 1:3, 1 John 2:29, 3:9, 4:7, 5:1-4, 18). John 1:12-13 indicates that being "born again" also carries the idea of "becoming children of God" through trust in the name of Jesus Christ.

The question logically comes, "Why does a person need to be born again?" The apostle Paul in Ephesians 2:1 says, "And you, he made alive, who were dead in trespasses and sins" (NKJV). To the Romans, he wrote, "For all have sinned and fall short of the glory of God" (Romans 3:23). Sinners are spiritually "dead" but, when they receive spiritual life through faith in Christ, the Bible likens it to a rebirth. Only those who are born again have their sins forgiven and have a relationship with God.

How does that come to be? Ephesians 2:8-9 states, "For it is by grace you have been saved, through faith—and this not from yourselves, it is the gift of God—not by works, so that no one can boast." When one is saved, he/she has been born again, spiritually renewed, and is now a child of God by right of a new birth. Trusting in Jesus Christ, the One who paid the penalty of sin when He died on the cross is the means to be "born again."

"Therefore, if anyone is in Christ, he is a new creation: the old has gone, the new has come!" (2 Corinthians 5:17).

"Yet to all who received him, to those who believed in His name, he gave the right to become children of God; children born not of natural descent, nor of human decision or a husband's will, but born of God" (John 1:12-13).

When visited by the religious leader Nicodemus, Jesus did not immediately assure him of heaven. Instead, Christ told him he had to become a child of God, saying, "I tell you the truth, no one can see the kingdom of God unless he is born again" (John 3:3).

The first time a person is born, he inherits the sinful nature that stems from Adam's disobedience in the Garden of Eden. No one has to teach a child how to sin. He naturally follows his own wrongful desires, leading to such sins as lying, stealing, and hating. Rather than being a child of God, he is a child of disobedience and wrath (Ephesians 2:1–3).

As children of wrath, we deserve to be separated from God in hell. Thankfully, Ephesians 2:4–5 says, "But because of his great love for us, God, who is rich in mercy, made us alive with Christ, even when we were dead in transgressions—it is by grace you have been saved." How are we made alive with Christ? By being born again and made a child of God. We must receive Jesus by faith!

"To all who have received him, those who believe in his name, he has given the right to become God's children," (John 1:12, NET). This verse clearly explains how to become a child of God. We must receive Jesus by believing in Him.

What must we believe about Jesus? First, the child of God recognizes that Jesus is the eternal Son of God, who became man. Born of a virgin through the power of the Holy Spirit, Jesus did not inherit Adam's sinful nature. Through Jesus, who is called the second Adam, all will be made alive (1 Corinthians 15:22). While Adam's disobedience brought the curse of sin on the world, Christ's perfect obedience brings a blessing. Our response must be to repent (turn from sin), and seek forgiveness in Christ.

Second, the child of God has faith in Jesus as Savior. God's plan was to sacrifice His perfect Son on the cross to pay the punishment we deserve for our sin; death. Christ's death frees those who receive Him from the penalty and power of sin. His resurrection justifies us (Romans 4:25).

Finally, the child of God follows Jesus as Lord. After raising up Christ as the Victor over sin and death, God gave Him all authority (Ephesians 1:20–23). Jesus leads all who receive Him; He will judge all who reject Him (Acts 10:42). By God's grace, we're born again into a new life as God's child. <u>Only those who receive Jesus, not merely knowing about Him but relying on Him for salvation, submitting to Him as Master, and loving Him as the supreme treasure—become children of God</u>.

Just as we had no part in our natural birth, <u>we cannot be born into God's family by just doing good deeds or conjuring up faith on our own</u>. God is the one who "gave the right" to become a child of God according to His gracious will. "How great is the love the Father has lavished on us, that we should be called children of God!" (1 John 3:1). Thus, the child of God has nothing to be proud about; his only boast is in the Lord (Ephesians 2:8–9).

A child grows up to look like his parents. Similarly, God wants His children to become more and more like Jesus Christ. Although, only in heaven will we be perfect, a child of God will not habitually, unrepentantly sin. "Dear children, do not let anyone lead you astray. **He who does what is right is righteous, just as he is righteous**. He who does what is sinful is of the devil, because the devil has been sinning from the beginning. The reason the Son of God appeared was to destroy the devil's work.

No one who is born of God will continue to sin, because God's seed remains in him; he cannot go on sinning, because he has been born of God. This is how we know who the children of God are and who the children of the devil are: Anyone who does not do what is right is not a child of God; nor is anyone who does not love his brother" (1 John 3:7–10).

To the Romans, Paul wrote in 3:23 "For all have sinned and fall short of the glory of God". Therefore, if anyone is in Christ, <u>he is a new creation</u>: the old has gone, the new has come! "Children of God are born <u>not of national descent, nor of human decision or a husband's will, but born of God</u>" (John 1:12-13).

1 Peter 1:23 - "For you have been born again, not of perishable (that decay) seed, but of imperishable, through the living and enduring word of God". In Titus 3:5-6, Paul declares "<u>He saved us through the washing of rebirth and renewal by the Holy Spirit</u>, whom he poured out on us generously through Jesus Christ our Savior."

— —

In John 3:3-7 Jesus is saying **that to be Born Again is to be Saved and you will see the kingdom of God.**

Our third step is receiving the Holy Spirit and instantly you become Born Again/Reborn/A New Creation:

One sign that you received the Holy Spirit, is the presence of one or more of the fruits of the Holy Spirit that are found in 1 Corinthians 12:8-10 below. Another is you began to notice a change in the way you see the world. An additional sign would be where you notice God is speaking to you and giving directions. Another way is speaking in tongues through the Holy Spirit. One dominant sign is the ability to know false teachings and false doctrines.

1 Corinthians 12:8-10 - To one, there is given through the Spirit a message of wisdom; to another, a message of knowledge by means of the same Spirit; [9] to another, faith by the same Spirit; to another, the gifts of healing by that one Spirit; [10] to another, miraculous powers; to another, prophecy; to another, distinguishing between spirits; to another, speaking in different kinds of tongues; and to still another, the interpretation of tongues.

Our fourth and final step:

Our fourth step would be to get baptized by a recognized Bible Church. Your baptism is a public declaration that shows positively your commitment to Jesus Christ.

Acts 2:38 - Peter replied, "Repent and be baptized, every one of you, in the name of Jesus Christ for the forgiveness of your sins. And you will receive the gift of the Holy Spirit."

1 Peter 3:21 - …and this water symbolizes baptism that now saves you also—not the removal of dirt from the body but the pledge of a clear conscience toward God. It saves you by the resurrection of Jesus Christ.

Acts 22:16 - And now what are you waiting for? Get up, be baptized, and wash your sins away, calling on his name.

Matthew 28:19-20 **Jesus said; Therefore go and make disciples of all nations, baptizing them in the name of the Father and of the Son and of the Holy Spirit, 20 and teaching them to obey everything I have commanded you.**

CHAPTER 5

WHO IS THE HOLY SPIRIT? WHAT IS KNOWN ABOUT THE HUMAN SPIRIT AND SOUL-GOD GIVES US?

The Holy Spirit in the Bible also goes by the name 'Spirit of the Lord', 'the Spirit of God', and 'Spirit'.

The Holy Spirit is described in Scripture as an invisible force, a dove, like the wind and appearing like tongues.

The Holy Spirit in the Old Testament was temporarily

Some of those who received the Holy Spirit in the Old Testament include;

Exodus 31:1-6 - Bezalel, who was giving the Holy Spirit, and given the instant knowledge to construct the Meeting Place (The Tabernacle), other furnishings, and the Ark of the Covenant. Bezalel received wisdom, understanding, and skills. With this gift, Bezalel became an expert in working with gold, silver, bronze, wood, cutting stone, and all kinds of crafts. This gift was also given to Oholiab, who would be his assistant.

When the Holy Spirit came upon Saul he was a changed man;

1 Samuel 10:6 - The Spirit of the Lord will come powerfully upon you, and you will prophesy with them; and you will be changed into a different person.

When the Holy Spirit is grieved it can depart from that person, like it did when Saul was King.

1 Samuel 16:14 - Now the Spirit of the Lord had departed from Saul, and an evil spirit from the Lord tormented him.

King Solomon and King David had the Holy Spirit. All authors of the Old Testament books were under the power/influence of the Holy Spirit when writing those books. The prophets and some of the kings also received the Holy Spirit. God also gave 70 Elders the same Spirit that Moses had and they prophesized. Others include Gideon the prophet and judge, and military leader Jephthah, and judge and warrior Samson.

The Holy Spirit at work in the Old Testament

Genesis 1:2
Now the earth was formless and empty, darkness was over the surface of the deep, and the [Holy] Spirit of God was hovering over the waters.

Psalms 104:30
When you send your Spirit, they are created, and you renew the face of the ground.

Isaiah 11:2
The Spirit of the Lord will rest on him—the Spirit of wisdom and of understanding, the Spirit of counsel and of might, the Spirit of the knowledge and fear of the Lord.

Some people who received the Holy Spirit in the New Testament

When Jesus spoke, Saul was blinded (now known as Apostle Paul) on the road to Damascus. The men with Saul fall into a state of shock, heard a sound, but didn't hear anyone talking to Saul, nor could they see anyone. However, they knew something extraordinary had happened. At Damascus, the blind Saul prayed and did not eat for three days. In a vision, Jesus told Ananias to lay his hands on Saul, and as he did the Holy Spirit cured him of his blindness and Saul received the Holy Spirit.

This is a rare example of a man who was persecuting the followers of Jesus, who didn't ask for the Holy Spirit or to follow Jesus. However, God knows a man's heart. Paul became one of the greatest human beings (with the help of the Holy Spirit) to ever live, the greatest was Jesus Christ. Paul wrote more than half of the New Testament under the inspiration (the power) of the Holy Spirit.

The apostles received the Holy Spirit. When Peter and John laid hands on the believers of Samaria they received the Holy Spirit. Cornelius was a commander in the Roman military and those in his household were the first Gentiles (first non-Jewish people) to receive the Holy Spirit.

The Holy Spirit helps us in the following areas

John 14:26 is about teaching all things.

Acts 1:8 gives you power.

1 John 2:20 with the Holy Spirit **you know the truth.**

Ephesians 1:13-14 marks you with a seal guaranteeing your inheritance. You become controlled by the Holy Spirit not sinful desires, the Holy Spirit pleads your case by using your voice and uses a prayer language that enables you to communicate with God, gives you talents to accomplish the tasks that God wants you to do.

Romans 8:26-27 helps us in our weaknesses, helps us to pray, and intercedes for us.

John 16:13 - But when he, the Spirit of truth, comes, he will guide you into all the truth. He will not speak on his own; he will speak only what he hears, and he will tell you what is yet to come.

In the last days, many will prophesize

Acts 2:17-18 - In the last days, God says, I will pour out my Spirit on all people. Your sons and daughters will prophesy, your young men will see visions, your old men will dream dreams. Even on my servants, both men and women, I will pour out my Spirit in those days, and they will prophesy.

Some are given the gift to Speak in Tongues

1 Corinthians 12:10 - To another, miraculous powers; to another, prophecy; to another, distinguishing between spirits; to another, speaking in different kinds of tongues, and to still another, the interpretation of tongues.

1 Corinthians 13:8 - Love never fails. But where there are prophecies, they will cease; where there are tongues, they will be stilled; where there is knowledge, it will pass away.

1 Corinthians 14:4 - Anyone who speaks in a tongue edifies themselves, but the one who prophesies edifies the church.

1 Corinthians 14:26-33 - What then shall we say, brothers and sisters? When you come together, each of you has a hymn, or a word of instruction, a revelation, a tongue, or an interpretation. Everything must be done so that the church may be built up. If anyone speaks in a tongue, two, or at the most three, should speak one at a time, and someone must interpret.

Verse 28 - If there is no interpreter, the speaker should keep quiet in the church and speak to himself and to God. Two or three prophets should speak, and the others should weigh carefully what is said. And if a revelation comes to someone who is sitting down, the first speaker should stop. For you can all prophesy in turns so that everyone may be instructed and encouraged. The spirits of prophets are subject to the control of prophets. For God is not a God of disorder but of peace, as in all the congregations of the Lord's people.

The Holy Spirit is free to those who ask. Here are two of the most important Scriptures in the Bible:

Luke 11:13 - **Jesus said, "If you then, though you are evil, know how to give good gifts to your children, how much more will your Father in heaven give the Holy Spirit to those who ask him!**

Acts 2:38-39 - **Peter replied, Repent and be baptized, every one of you, in the name of Jesus Christ for the forgiveness of your sins. And you will receive the gift of the Holy Spirit."**

You can receive the gift of the Holy Spirit!!!

The Human Soul

The Human Soul is real; helps leads you to God, helps you to love God, to live, and the Human Soul is owned/belongs to God.

Deuteronomy 4:29 - But if from there you seek the Lord your God, you will find him if you seek him with all your heart and with all your soul.

Deuteronomy 26:16 - The Lord your God commands you this day to follow these decrees and laws; carefully observe them with all your heart and with all your soul.

Deuteronomy 30:6 - The Lord your God will circumcise your hearts and the hearts of your descendants, so that you may love him with all your heart and with all your soul, and live.

Psalms 19:7 - The law of the Lord is perfect, refreshing the soul. The statutes of the Lord are trustworthy, making wise the simple.

Psalms 62:1 - Truly, my soul finds rest in God; my salvation comes from him.

Joshua 22:5 - But be very careful to keep the commandment and the law that Moses the servant of the Lord gave you: to love the Lord your God, to walk in obedience to him, to keep his commands, to hold fast to him and to serve him with all your heart and with all your soul.

Hebrews 4:12 - For the word of God is alive and active. Sharper than any double-edged sword, it penetrates even to dividing soul and spirit, joints and marrow; it judges the thoughts and attitudes of the heart.

Ezekiel 18:4 - "Behold, all souls are mine; the soul of the father as well as the soul of the son is mine: the soul who sins shall die" (ESV Bible).

Matthew 10:28 - Do not be afraid of those who kill the body but cannot kill the soul. Rather, be afraid of the One who can destroy both soul and body in hell.

16:26 - What good will it be for someone to gain the whole world, yet forfeit their soul? Or what can anyone give in exchange for their soul?

22:37 - Jesus replied, Love the Lord your God with all your heart and with all your soul and with all your mind.

Human Spirit

The Human Spirit verifies you are children of God; gives understanding, knows your thoughts, and when you die your spirit returns to God.

Romans 8:16 - "The Spirit himself testifies with your spirit that we are God's children".

Romans 1:9 - God, whom I serve in my spirit in preaching the gospel of his Son, is my witness to how constantly I remember you.

Job 32:8 - But it is the spirit in a person, the breath of the Almighty, that gives them understanding.

Proverbs 20:27 - The human spirit is the lamp of the Lord that sheds light on one's inmost being.

Ecclesiastes 12:7 - and the dust returns to the ground it came from, and the spirit returns to God who gave it.

1 Corinthians 2:11 - For who knows a person's thoughts except their own spirit within them? In the same way, no one knows the thoughts of God except the Spirit of God.

Romans 8:16 - The Spirit himself <u>testifies with our spirit that we are God's children.</u>

Luke 23:46 - Jesus called out with a loud voice, "Father, into your hands I commit my spirit." When he had said this, he breathed his last.

1 Thessalonians 5:23 - May God himself, the God of peace, sanctify you through and throug<u>h. May your whole spirit, soul, and body be kept blameless</u> at the coming of our Lord Jesus Christ.

Hebrews 4:12 - For the word of God is alive and active. Sharper than any double-edged sword, it penetrates even to dividing soul and spirit, joints and marrow; <u>it judges the thoughts and attitudes of the heart.</u>

James 2:26 - As the body without the spirit is dead, so faith without deeds is dead.

CHAPTER 6

FALSE RELIGIONS THAT DON'T FOLLOW THE TRUE GOD

Note: This chapter (with the exception of the highlighted comments) comes from the book "False Facts on False Teachings" by Ron Carlson and Ed Decker-with his permission. The Catholic Church section is separate.

Below is a list of some of the false religions. They're false because they do not follow Scripture thoroughly. Some accept parts of Scripture and then incorporate man-made rules in them, which become traditions.

All these religions rely on good works to be saved; whereas <u>True Bible Church's</u> rely on the grace of God, as found in the Scriptures, and they do not add or subtract from the Scriptures.

People follow false religions because they don't know the Scriptures and see their church leaders, or pope, as the person who determines what is right and acceptable. Others follow false religions because it doesn't require much effort from them, and what is discussed in these religions is fun and entertaining to them.

The False Teachings of Atheism, Buddhism, Hindu, Yoga, Reincarnation and the New Age Movement:

Atheism

Atheist people believe that there is no God. However, it's impossible to have this belief, since they don't have infinite knowledge, and their god is whoever they put their efforts in life to support - like in evolution, material things, the devil, one's own family, etc.

Romans 1:18-25 - The wrath of God is being revealed from heaven against all the godlessness and wickedness of people, who suppress the truth by their wickedness, [19] since what may be known about God is

plain to them because God has made it plain to them. [20] For, since the creation of the world, God's invisible qualities, his eternal power and divine nature, have been clearly seen; being understood from what has been made, so that people are without excuse.

[21] <u>For, although they knew God, they neither glorified him as God nor gave thanks</u> to him, but their thinking became futile and their foolish hearts were darkened.

[22] <u>Although they claimed to be wise, they became fools,</u> [23] and exchanged the glory of the immortal God for images made to look like a mortal human being and birds and animals and reptiles.

²⁴ <u>Therefore God gave them over in the sinful desires of their hearts to sexual impurity for the degrading of their bodies with one another</u>. ²⁵ They exchanged the truth about God for a lie, and worshiped and served created things, rather than the Creator who is forever praised. Amen.

Man always finds something to worship. Man has an innate spiritual desire (implanted by the Creator) to worship the true God or false gods-wooded/stone idols, money, and so-called sophisticated civilization, etc.

Atheism is not a valid philosophy. It is intellectually bankrupt and demonstrates a willful denial of all that God has revealed.

John 3:16-17 - For God so loved the world that he gave his one and only Son, <u>that whoever believes in him shall not perish but have eternal life</u>. ¹⁷ For God did not send his Son into the world to condemn the world, but to save the world through him.

Buddhism

Buddha means "the enlightened one". The founder Siddhartha (Sid-dar-ta), Gautama, lived in about 563 to 483 BC. He was born into a wealthy Hindu family in the hill country boarding India and Nepal.

Basics of Buddhism:

1. Life is about suffering.

2. Suffering is caused by desire.

3. The cessation of desire eliminates suffering.

4. The stopping of desire comes by following the "Middle Way"; avoiding the extremes of self-denial and self-indulgence.

The goal of human existence is to free oneself from the "Law of Karma", "Cause and Effect" of good and bad deeds and achieve the state of "Nirvana"; where one ceases desiring and thus eliminates suffering.

Buddha was an Atheist. He did not believe in God and felt that the very concept of God or gods was holding people bound to this physical world of Karma and suffering.

Buddha condemned idolatry, yet became a major part of Buddhism, with its many shrines and statues of Buddha. In Sri Lanka, the city of Kandy is the Temple of the Tooth, which has a tooth of Buddha; where people gather and bring flowers and rice as offerings, bow down and worship, and pray to a gold box decorated with jewels, that has the tooth of Buddha. Buddhism religion has thousands of wood, stone, and metal statues.

Romans 1:22-23 - Although they claimed to be wise, they became fools [23] and exchanged the glory of the immortal God for images made to look like a mortal human being and birds and animals and reptiles.

Jeremiah 10:3-5 - For the practices of the peoples are worthless; they cut a tree out of the forest, and a craftsman shapes it with his chisel. [4] They adorn it with silver and gold; they fasten it with hammer and nails so it will not totter. Like a scarecrow in a cucumber field, their idols cannot speak; they must be carried because they cannot walk. Do not fear them; they can do no harm nor can they do any good.

The use of yoga has its roots in Buddhism, and can also be found in Hinduism and Jainism.

Stay away from this idolatry practice of Yoga; it has its roots in paganism. Like other things that aren't good for Christians, it can lead you astray. Yoga exercises encourage you to clear your mind of all thoughts, thus opening a door for evil spirits.

Hinduism, Yoga, and Reincarnation:

Instead of using drugs, men can alter their consciousness through yoga and Hindu forms of meditation, such as Transcendental Meditation.

Hinduism and Buddhism parallel Evolution and Humanism by offering a continuum of evolution; not only did man evolve from slimy algae, but he can continue his evolution through cycles of rebirth, which is known as reincarnation.

Monism is the Hindu philosophy that says we are one with nature, one with the universe, and one with all living things.

The ultimate goal of Hinduism and Buddhism is to liberate ourselves from this "physical personal existence", and become one with the "impersonal all" <u>by not having or showing feelings</u>. In Hinduism, this "impersonal all" is often referred to as Brahman-Atman or the true reality.

Therefore, you must transcend this physical existence and be absorbed into this "true reality". This is accomplished <u>by means of yoga or transcendental meditation</u>; the main vehicles for transcending this world of illusion.

The problem with an impersonal universe is that it destroys personality and all the characteristics that make us human:

1. An impersonal society never loves or cares about anyone.

2. A Hindu swami or Buddhist monk in India or Southeast Asia is known as a "parasite". He does nothing for the people. He exists by begging and living off others while renouncing the material world.

3. There is no basis for morality. Since all is One, what could be bad?

4. An impersonal world eliminates human will and freedom of choice because a person's position in life is a result of one's karma in a past life. Karma is the Hindu teaching that actions in one's life will determine a person's fate in the next cycle of life.

Thus, fatalism dominates countries like India and those in Southeast Asia.

<u>Fatalism is the belief that events are fixed in advance for all time, in such a way that human beings are powerless to change them</u>. Fatalism destroys any desire for human achievement in life, since everything is already predetermined by fate.

Reincarnation

Hinduism and Buddhism teach that based on the Law of Karma, your good and bad deeds will determine how you will come back in your next life. If you lived a bad life and did not renounce this world of illusion you may come back at a lower form of life.

The possibilities of returning as a cow or rat have made both animals sacred in India.

You don't kill a rat or a cow because it might be someone's aunt or uncle reincarnated. The United Nations estimates there are three times more rats in India than the human population. These rats eat nearly one-fourth of the total grain crop!

The Hindu leader Vivkan Anda visited the United States and discovered that Americans were not very excited about the Hinduism belief of coming back as a rat, a frog, or a snail. So, the concept of reincarnation was changed to where you could only come back as another human being.

Everyone who believes in reincarnation, whether New Agers, Hinduism, or Buddhism, all deny a personal creator. They believe that we are part of an impersonal universe.

True Christians don't need reincarnation;

1. Christians can have a personal relationship with God.

2. The blood sacrifice of Jesus Christ on the cross covered over our sins as an ultimate payment.

3. Jesus Christ resurrection did away with automatic death for our sins, **if we get saved and follow Him.**

John 11:25-26 - Jesus said to her, "I am the resurrection and the life. The one who believes in me will live, even though they die; ²⁶ and whoever lives by believing in me will never die. Do you believe this?"

Hebrews 9:27 - Just as people are destined to die once, and after that to face judgment (shows we are not reincarnated).

The New Age Movement

The serpent said in Genesis 3:1:6, "Now the serpent was craftier than any of the wild animals the Lord God had made." He said to the woman, "Did God really say you must not eat from any tree in the garden?"

² The woman said to the serpent, "We may eat fruit from the trees in the garden, ³ but God did say, 'You must not eat fruit from the tree that is in the middle of the garden, and you must not touch it, or you will die.' "

⁴ "You will not certainly die," the serpent said to the woman. ⁵ "For God knows that when you eat from it your eyes will be opened, and you will be like God, knowing good and evil."

⁶ When the woman saw that the fruit of the tree was good for food and pleasing to the eye, and also desirable for gaining wisdom, she took some and ate it. She also gave some to her husband, who was with her, and he ate it.

New Age teaches;

1. God's Word cannot be trusted entirely (verses 1, 4, and 5).

2. Man does not have to die (verse 4).

3. Man can become a god (verse 5).

4. Man can evolve through hidden knowledge (verse 6).

New Age definitions:

1. God - no personal God at all just a cosmic force, a fragment of which is in us; therefore we are gods.

2. Jesus - a man who evolved into an ascended master (god-like being) through occult and metaphysical disciplines.

3. Christ - an impersonal "force" that rested in the man Jesus.

4. The Bible - at best a work of cabalistic (associated with or related to mystical interpretations) secrets.

5. Salvation - by works of the occult discipline. The law of Karma is irresistible and is what judges us.

Roots of the New Age:

A. Witchcraft and Shamanism. A shaman interacts with what they believe to be a spirit world.

B. Astrology (2000 BC).

C. Hinduism and yoga (1800 BC).

The New Age came into existence in the 1980s. There is no single leader and no single organization.

2 Corinthians 4:4 - The god of this age has blinded the minds of unbelievers so that they cannot see the light of the gospel of the glory of Christ, who is the image of God.

In 1980 the New Age is movement became enmeshed in every area of society:

1. Public Education has become heavily New Age influenced. The public schools' instructions include New Age-oriented classes and acceptance programs.

Children, all the way down to the first grade, are being taught to lay on the floor and practice visualization, guided imagery, yoga, and meditation. They are told "to go within" and tap their own divine energy.

2. Corporations use their techniques for executive training.

3. Political and military leaders push it.

4. The United Nations promotes it.

5. Many **false** churches teach New Age concepts; belief in reincarnation, astrology, psychics, and the presence of spiritual energy in physical objects.

2 Titus 4:3-4 - The time will come when they will not endure sound doctrine, but according to their own desires, because they have itching ears, they will heap up for themselves teachers; and they will turn their ears away from the truth, and be turned aside to fables.

Romans 1:21-32 - For although they knew God, they neither glorified him as God nor gave thanks to him, but their thinking became futile and their foolish hearts were darkened. [22] Although they claimed to be wise, they became fools [23] and exchanged the glory of the immortal God for images made to look like a mortal human being and birds and animals and reptiles.

[24] Therefore God gave them over in the sinful desires of their hearts to sexual impurity for the degrading of their bodies with one another. [25] They exchanged the truth about God for a lie, and worshiped and served created things rather than the Creator who is forever praised. Amen.

Because of this, God gave them over to shameful lusts. Even their women exchanged natural sexual relations for unnatural ones. [27] In the same way the men also abandoned natural relations with women and were inflamed with lust for one another. Men committed shameful acts with other men, and received in themselves the due penalty for their error.

[28] Furthermore, just as they did not think it worthwhile to retain the knowledge of God, so, God gave them over to a depraved mind, so that they do what ought not to be done. [29] They have become filled with every kind of wickedness, evil, greed, and depravity. They are full of envy, murder, strife, deceit, and malice. They are gossipers, slanderers, God-haters, insolent, arrogant, and boastful; they invent ways of doing evil; they disobey their parents; [31] they have no understanding, no fidelity, no love, and no mercy.

[32] Although they know God's righteous decree that those who do such things deserve death, they not only continue to do these very things but also approve of those who practice them.

In 1975 Maharishi Mahesh Yogi, founder of Transcendental Meditation, was on the Merv Griffin Show; Clint Eastwood came out with a bouquet of flowers and bowed at his feet, then out came Burt Reynolds with flowers and he bowed at Yogi's feet, then Mary Tyler Moore bowed at his feet. All three claimed to have found peace and fulfillment through Hindu Meditation. To their many millions of fans, this was a revelation from the gods.

Scriptures on bowing (showing respect for an ungodly make-believe holy figure):

Exodus 20:4-6 - You shall not make for yourself an image in the form of anything in heaven above or on the earth beneath or in the waters below. [5] You shall not bow down to them or worship them; for I, the Lord your God, am a jealous God, punishing the children for the sin of the parents to the third and fourth generation of those who hate me, [6] but showing love to a thousand generations of those who love me and keep my commandments.

Leviticus 26:1 - Do not make idols or set up an image or a sacred stone for yourselves, and do not place a carved stone in your land to bow down before it. I am the Lord your God.

Deuteronomy 5:8-10 - You shall not make for yourself an image in the form of anything in heaven above or on the earth beneath or in the waters below. [9] You shall not bow down to them or worship them; for I, the Lord your God, am a jealous God, punishing the children for the sin of the parents to the third and fourth generation of those who hate me, [10] but showing love to a thousand generations of those who love me and keep my commandments.

Matthew 4:4-9 Jesus answered, 'Man shall not live on bread alone, but on every word that comes from the mouth of God.' Then the devil took him to the holy city and had him stand on the highest point of the temple. ⁶ If you are the Son of God, he said, throw yourself down.

For it is written: "'He will command his angels concerning you, and they will lift you up in their hands so that you will not strike your foot against a stone.'"⁷ Jesus answered him, "It is also written: 'Do not put the Lord your God to the test.'" Jesus answered him, "It is also written: 'Do not put the Lord your God to the test.'"

⁸ Again, the devil took him to a very high mountain and showed him all the kingdoms of the world and their splendor. ⁹ "All this I will give you," he said, "if you will bow down and worship me."

Romans 14:11 - It is written: "'As surely as I live, 'says the Lord, 'every knee will bow before me; every tongue will acknowledge God.'"

Revelation 19:10 - At this I fell at his feet to worship him. But he said to me, "Don't do that! I am a fellow servant with you and with your brothers and sisters who hold to the testimony of Jesus. Worship God! For it is the Spirit of prophecy who bears testimony to Jesus.

Scripture says you will bow eventually to Jesus.

Philippians 2:9-11 - Therefore God exalted him to the highest place and gave him the name that is above every name, ¹⁰ that, at the name of Jesus, every knee should bow, in heaven and on earth and under the earth, ¹¹ and every tongue should acknowledge that Jesus Christ is Lord, to the glory of God the Father.

The False Teachings of the Freemasonry And the Masonic Lodge

The journey into Freemasonry begins at what is known as "The Blue Lodge" which is the foundation of all Freemasonry. In the Blue Lodge, there are three degrees; the Entered Apprentice Degree, then the Fellow-craft Degree, and then the Master Mason Degree.

After completion of these degrees, the Mason has a choice of staying in the Blue Lodge or advancing through either the Scottish Rite or York Rite.

Once the mason has attained the Thirty-Second Degree, he has the option of petitioning to join the Shriners.

When degrees are completed in the Blue Lodge, Scottish or York Rites, Masonry enter what is known as "The Ancient and Arabic Order of the Mystic Shrine."

Every Mason who joins the Lodge takes his thumb or his hand to his throat and repeats an oath:

The Oath for the Blue Lodge: "Binding myself under no less a penalty than having my throat cut across my tongue and torn out by its roots, and buried in the rough sands of the sea..."

In the Fellowship Degree, this oath is: "Binding myself under no less a penalty than that of having my left breast torn open, my heart plucked out and given as prey to the wild beasts of the fields and the fowls of the air…"

Then in the Third Degree or the Master Mason's Degree, every Mason swears this oath:

"Binding myself under no less a penalty than that of having my body severed in twain, my bowels taken from thence and buried in ashes."

Then they come before a leader called the 'Worshipful Master', and bow before him in a religious ceremony and say, "I am lost in the darkness."

Matthew 6:24 - No one can serve two masters. Either you will hate the one and love the other, or you will be devoted to the one and despise the other. You cannot serve both God and money.

The secret pagan blood oaths of secrecy:

They bow down in ignorance of the secrets to which they are being bound too, and knell blindfolded in a lodge room, with a noose around their neck and swearing obedience to things the person has no understanding of.

Mason scholar, Steinmetz writes, "The average Mason is lamentably [deplorably] ignorant of the real meaning of the Masonic symbols, and knows little of its esoteric [known to only a few] teachings.

The goal of each Masonry, according to its leading authorities, is to do away with religions and their creeds and doctrines, and to establish a one-world, universal religion, free from the confining dogma of such narrow scope, as is found in Christianity.

The first secret of the Lodge is the fact that Freemasonry is a religion. Masonry only requires the new member to have a belief in any god.

Romans 1:21-25 - For although they knew God, they neither glorified him as God nor gave thanks to him, but their thinking became futile and their foolish hearts were darkened. [22] Although they claimed to be wise, they became fools [23] and exchanged the glory of the immortal God for images made to look like a mortal human being and birds and animals and reptiles.

[24] Therefore God gave them over in the sinful desires of their hearts to sexual impurity for the degrading of their bodies with one another. [25] They exchanged the truth about God for a lie, and worshiped and served created things rather than the Creator, who is forever praised. Amen.

Some believe that the first Masonic teacher was Buddha.

"The Mason recognizes only the light and not the bearer. He worships at every shrine, bows before every altar, whether in the temple, mosque or cathedral" says, the author of The Lost Keys of Freemasonry.

More scriptures on bowing down to ungodly figures

Exodus 20:1-5 - And God spoke all these words: [2] I am the Lord your God, who brought you out of Egypt, out of the land of slavery. [3] You shall have no other gods before me. [4] "You shall not make for yourself an image in the form of anything in heaven above or on the earth beneath or in the waters below. [5] You shall not bow down to them or worship them; for I, the Lord your God, am a jealous God, punishing the children for the sin of the parents to the third and fourth generation of those who hate me.

Exodus 23:24 - <u>Do not bow down before their gods or worship them or follow their practices</u>. You must demolish them and break their sacred stones to pieces.

Deuteronomy 5:9 - <u>You shall not bow down to them or worship them</u>; for I, the Lord your God, am a jealous God, punishing the children for the sin of the parents to the third and fourth generation of those who hate me.

The Bible tells us that Jesus is the only way we can be saved:

1 Timothy 2:5 - For there is one God and one mediator between God and mankind, the man Christ Jesus.

Acts 4:12 - Salvation is found in no one else, for there is no other name under heaven given to mankind by which we must be saved.

Oaths and Swearing in the Bible:

Matthew 5:33-37 - Again, you have heard that it was said to the people long ago, 'Do not break your oath, but fulfill to the Lord the vows you have made.'[34] But I tell you, do not swear an oath at all; either by heaven, for it is God's throne; [35] or by the earth, for it is his footstool; or by Jerusalem, for it is the city of the Great King. [36] And do not swear by your head, for you cannot make even one hair white or black. [37] All you need to say is simply 'Yes' or 'No'; anything beyond this comes from the evil one.

James 5:12 - Above all, my brothers and sisters, do not swear—not by heaven or by earth or by anything else. All you need to say is a simple "Yes" or "No." Otherwise, you will be condemned.

Through all thirty-three degrees of Freemasonry, every Mason in the world is bound by bloody oaths to maintain the secrets of the Lodge. The penalties for the brethren of the Lodge include serious physical harm.

In the seventeenth degree of the Scottish Rite or the Knights of the East and West Degree, they are given the secret password "Jubulum" and the sacred word "Abaddon".

Revelation 9:11 - They had, as king, over them the angel of the Abyss, whose name in Hebrew is Abaddon and in Greek is Apollyon (that is, Destroyer).

What is represented as the god of Masonry is a three-headed monster.

2 Corinthian 6:14-17 - Do not be yoked together with unbelievers. For what do righteousness and wickedness have in common? Or what fellowship can light have with darkness? [15] What harmony is there between Christ and Belial? Or what does a believer have in common with an unbeliever? [16] What agreement is there between the temple of God and idols? For we are the temple of the living God.

As God has said, "I will live with them and walk among them, and I will be their God, and they will be my people." Therefore, "Come out from them and be separate, says the Lord. Touch no unclean thing, and I will receive you."

GOD HAS A PLAN

TRUST IT. LIVE IT. PLAN IT

Roman Catholic Church

CCC stands for the second and latest edition of "Catechism of the Catholic Church". This book consolidates all the churches' beliefs that are referenced by CCC paragraph numbers in this section.

1.   **The Church was built on Peter** who is called the first Pope

Jesus used the term rock for Peter which is called in the Greek "Petros" which means a stone or small rock. When Jesus said, "On this rock, I will build my church", the rock here is expressed in Greek as "Petra", which means massive stone, a foundation stone, a bedrock. In reality, Jesus was saying Peter you are a small stone, but it is upon this stone, the Petra (Jesus), that I am going to build my church.

Peter never gave orders to the other apostles; rather we find Peter was sent by others as in;

Acts 8:14 - When the apostles in Jerusalem heard that Samaria had accepted the word of God, they sent Peter and John to Samaria.

Paul rebuked the Apostle Peter, who Jesus called Cephas;

Galatians 2:11 - When Cephas came to Antioch, I opposed him to his face, because he stood condemned.

This Scripture shows that Peter was not over Paul.

-The apostle's gatherings and churches were run independently.

-The church after the first 100 years had bishops, not popes.

-Jesus never said or implied that Peter would be the head of the new religion (first called the Way then changed to Christianity).

1 Corinthians 3:11 - **For no one can lay any foundation other than the one already laid, which is Jesus Christ**

The above Scripture and the two below, state very clearly that Jesus was the foundation (the Rock).

1 Corinthians 10:4 - and drank the same spiritual drink; for they drank from the spiritual rock that accompanied them, <u>and that rock was Christ.</u>

Ephesians 2:20 - built on the foundation of the apostles and prophets, <u>with Christ Jesus himself as the chief cornerstone.</u>

In the Old Testament God was always referred to as the Rock;

Psalm 18:2 - The Lord is my rock, my fortress, and my deliverer; my God is my rock, in whom I take refuge, my shield and the horn of my salvation, my stronghold.

Deuteronomy 32:4 - He is the Rock, his works are perfect, and all his ways are just. A faithful God who does no wrong, upright, and just is he.

1 Samuel 2:2 - There is no one holy like the Lord; there is no one besides you; there is no Rock like our God.

2. **Purgatory** is a made-up place where Catholics go after death to purify their sins. These are people who needed a little cleaning up before going to heaven. Scripture tells us that those who are Born Again in this life will automatically inherit eternal life.

CCC 1472, "…On the other hand <u>every sin, even venial, entails an unhealthy attachment to creatures, which must be purified either here on earth, or after death in the state called Purgatory.</u> This purification frees one from what is called the "temporal punishment" of sin …"

John 5:24 - Very truly I tell you, **whoever hears my word and believes him who sent me has eternal life and will not be judged,** but has crossed over from death to life.

1 Peter 1:23 - <u>For you have been born again, not of perishable seed, but of imperishable</u>, through the living and enduring word of God.

3. **Prayers to Mary and the dead saints**, so as to mediate on their behalf.

John 14:6 - Jesus answered, "I am the way and the truth and the life. <u>No one comes to the Father except through me."</u>

Acts 4:12 - <u>Salvation is found in no one else, for there is no other name under heaven given to mankind by which we must be saved.</u>

1 Timothy 2:5 - <u>For there is one God and one mediator between God and mankind, the man Christ Jesus.</u>

Matthew 6:9 - This, then, is how you should pray:

"Our Father in heaven, hallowed be your name, [10] your kingdom come, your will be done, on earth as it is in heaven. Give us today our daily bread. [12] And forgive us our debts, as we also have forgiven our debtors. And lead us not into temptation, but deliver us from the evil one."

The "Our Father Prayer" says pray to God and nobody else. Why would anyone want to pray to someone astronomically lower, with absolutely no power or authority? Go all the way to the top as instructed in many Scriptures.

In 2019 of June, Pope Francis changed the last part of the "Our Father Prayer", that says, "lead us not into temptation" to "do not let us fall into temptation". Apparently he thinks he knows more than the Creator of all things.

Isaiah 45:7 in the NIV states, "I form the light and create darkness". Other Bibles use the word disaster or evil instead of darkness. The Hebrew word for evil is adversity, affliction, calamity, distress and misery.

In Job chapter 1 verse [6]: One day the angels came to present themselves before the Lord, and Satan also came with them. [7] The Lord said to Satan, "Where have you come from?" Satan answered the Lord, "From roaming throughout the earth, going back and forth on it."

[8]Then the Lord said to Satan, "Have you considered my servant Job? There is no one on earth like him; he is blameless and upright, a man who fears God and shuns evil."

⁹"Does Job fear God for nothing?" Satan replied. ¹⁰ "Have you not put a hedge around him and his household and everything he has? You have blessed the work of his hands, so that his flocks and herds are spread throughout the land. 11 But now stretch out your hand and strike everything he has, and he will surely curse you to your face."

¹²The Lord said to Satan, <u>"Very well, then, everything he has is in your power, but on the man himself do not lay a finger."</u>

Then Satan went out from the presence of the Lord. ¹³One day when Job's sons and daughters were feasting and drinking wine at the oldest brother's house, ¹⁴a messenger came to Job and said, "The oxen were plowing and the donkeys were grazing nearby, ¹⁵and the Sabeans attacked and made off with them. They put the servants to the sword, and I am the only one who has escaped to tell you!"

¹⁶While he was still speaking, another messenger came and said, "The fire of God fell from the heavens and burned up the sheep and the servants, and I am the only one who has escaped to tell you!"

¹⁷While he was still speaking, another messenger came and said, "The Chaldeans formed three raiding parties and swept down on your camels and made off with them. They put the servants to the sword, and I am the only one who has escaped to tell you!"

¹⁸While he was still speaking, yet another messenger came and said, "Your sons and daughters were feasting and drinking wine at the oldest brother's house, ¹⁹when suddenly a mighty wind swept in from the desert and struck the four corners of the house. It collapsed on them and they are dead, and I am the only one who has escaped to tell you!"

²⁰At this, Job got up and tore his robe and shaved his head. Then he fell to the ground in worship.

Satan's power over Job was increased because God allowed it. Did Jobs' trial come from God or Satan? The immediate cause was Satan and the ultimate cause was God.

Note: in verse 16 "The fire of God fell from the heavens" the messenger should have said the fire came from Satan. In the last verse 20, notice how Job after losing all his children and all his livestock-he did not get angry, moan and cry-he praised God!

In 1 Samuel 16:14 Now the Spirit of the Lord had departed from Saul, and an evil spirit from the Lord tormented him. ¹⁵ Saul's attendants said to him, "See, an evil spirit from God is tormenting you.

The above Scripture is saying the Holy Spirit left King Saul because of his evil actions, and God lead him into temptation.

Romans 1:26-32 Because of this, God gave them over to shameful lusts. Even their women exchanged natural sexual relations for unnatural ones. ²⁷ In the same way the men also abandoned natural relations with women and were inflamed with lust for one another. Men committed shameful acts with other men, and received in themselves the due penalty for their error.

Matthew 4:1-4 <u>Then Jesus was led by the Spirit into the wilderness to be tempted by the devil</u>. ² After fasting forty days and forty nights, he was hungry. ³ The tempter came to him and said, If you are the Son of God, tell these stones to become bread.

⁴ Jesus answered, It is written: 'Man shall not live on bread alone, but on every word that comes from the mouth of God.

God himself lead his only begotten Son into temptation with the Holy Spirit.

God at times leads us into temptation, so we can repent and hopefully change. God wishes to save all of His creations.

In 1854, Pope Pius IX declared Mary was the Immaculate Conception; that Mary was free from sin unlike any other human being, and her bodily Assumption (alive) into heaven was declared by Pope Pius XII in 1950. The Catholic Church says Mary never died.

Mary is Mediatrix, CCC 969, "Therefore the Blessed Virgin is invoked in the Church under the titles of Advocate, Helper, Benefactress, and Mediatrix.'"

Mary brings us the gifts of eternal salvation, CCC 969, "Taken up to heaven she did not lay aside this saving office but by her manifold intercession continues to bring us the gifts of eternal salvation ..."

CCC 2677, "By asking Mary to pray for us, we acknowledge ourselves to be poor sinners and we address ourselves to the 'Mother of Mercy,' the All-Holy One. We give ourselves over to her now, in the Today of our lives. And our trust broadens further, already at the present moment, to surrender 'the hour of our death' wholly to her care."

Praying to the dead saints

CCC 1475, "In the communion of saints, "a perennial link of charity exists between the faithful who have already reached their heavenly home, those who are expiating their sins in purgatory, and those who are still pilgrims on the earth. Between them, there is, too, an abundant exchange of all good things." In this wonderful exchange, the holiness of one profits others, well beyond the harm that the sin of one could cause others. Thus recourse to the communion of saints lets the contrite sinner be more promptly and efficaciously purified of the punishments for sin.

Revelation 19:10 - [Apostle John speaking] "At this, I fell at his feet to worship him. But he said to me, 'don't do that! I am a fellow servant with you and with your brothers and sisters who hold to the testimony of Jesus. Worship God! For it is the Spirit of prophecy who bears testimony to Jesus.'"

In Luke 1:46-49, Mary herself recognizes her need for a savior;

[46] And Mary said, "My soul glorifies the Lord [47] and my spirit rejoices in God my Savior, [48] for he has been mindful of the humble state of his servant. From now on all generations will call me blessed, [49] for the Mighty One has done great things for me, holy is his name.

Matthew 12:46-50 - While Jesus was still talking to the crowd, his mother and brothers stood outside, wanting to speak to him. Someone told him, "Your mother and brothers are standing outside, wanting to speak to you." He replied to him, "Who is my mother, and who are my brothers?" Pointing to his disciples, he said, "Here are my mother and my brothers. For whoever does the will of my Father in heaven is my brother and sister and mother.

4.   Kneeling and praying before images

Acts 10:26 - [The Apostle Peter would not allow it] Peter made him get up. "Stand up," he said, "I am only a man myself."

Exodus 20:4 - You shall not make for yourself an image in the form of anything in heaven above or on the earth beneath or in the waters below.

Isaiah 44:9-11 - All who make idols are nothing, and the things they treasure are worthless. Those who would speak up for them are blind; they are ignorant, to their own shame. Who shapes a god and casts an idol, which can profit nothing? People who do that will be put to shame; such craftsmen are only human beings.

Let them all come together and take their stand; they will be brought down to terror and shame.

Venerate means to regard with great respect, revere, to worship, adore and honor.

Revere means to feel deep respect, admire, honor, esteem, and reverence.

Reverence means deep respect for someone or something.

5.   Confession to a priest for absolution (release from guilt or punishment) of sins

Isaiah 43:25 - I, even I, am he [God] who blots out your transgressions, for my own sake, and remembers your sins no more.

Mark 11:25 - And when you stand praying, if you hold anything against anyone, forgive them, <u>so that your Father in heaven may forgive you your sins</u>.

Psalm 32:5 - Then I acknowledged my sin to you and did not cover up my iniquity. I said, "I will confess my transgressions to the Lord." <u>And you forgave the guilt of my sin.</u>

Acts 8:22 - Repent of this wickedness <u>and pray to the Lord in the hope that he may forgive you</u> for having such a thought in your heart. We must confess our sins to one another not just privately to God. Yet, those people we confess to can forgive you for their own sake, <u>but only God can absolve (wipe out) your sins.</u>

James 5:16 - Therefore confess your sins to each other and pray for each other so that you may be healed. The prayer of a righteous person is powerful and effective.

Mark 2:5-7 - When Jesus saw their faith, he said to the paralyzed man, <u>"Son, your sins are forgiven."</u> [6] Now some teachers of the law were sitting there, thinking to themselves, [7] "Why does this fellow talk like that? He's blaspheming! <u>Who can forgive sins but God alone?</u>"

No human being or angel has the authority to blot out sins. A person you offended can forgive you, but only God can blot (wipe out) that sin from the record.

6. **Grace can be merited (by good works done).** This belief that grace can be merited <u>completely goes against</u> the grace of God as mentioned in the Scriptures below.

CCC 2010, "Moved by the Holy Spirit and by charity, <u>we can then merit for ourselves</u> and, for others, the graces needed for our sanctification."

CCC 2027, "Moved by the Holy Spirit, <u>we can merit for ourselves and for others all the graces needed to attain eternal life</u>, as well as necessary temporal goods."

CCC 1477, "This treasury includes as well the prayers and good works of the Blessed Virgin Mary. They are truly immense, unfathomable, and even pristine in their value before God. In the treasury, too, are the prayers and good works of all the saints, all those who have followed in the footsteps of Christ the Lord and by his grace have made their lives holy and carried out the mission in the unity of the Mystical Body."

The Scriptures below show that once you're Born Again you don't have to merit anything;

Romans 6:23 - For the wages of sin is death, but the gift of God is eternal life in Christ Jesus our Lord.

Ephesians 1:13-14 - And you also were included in Christ when you heard the message of truth, the gospel of your salvation. When you believed, you were marked in him with a seal, the promised Holy Spirit, [14] who is a deposit, guaranteeing our inheritance until the redemption of those who are God's possession, to the praise of his glory.

John 3:16 - For God so loved the world that he gave his one and only Son, that whoever believes in him shall not perish but have eternal life.

7.   The Roman Catholic Church says **the full benefit of Salvation** is only through them. As you'll see Salvation is the gift of God.

And stating the mass and sacraments are necessary for salvation and that salvation only comes through the Roman Catholic Church-Pope Boniface the Eight in his Bull of 1302 stated, "For every human creature, it is altogether necessary to salvation that he be subject to the Roman Pontiff."

"For it is only through Christ's Catholic Church, which is "the all-embracing means of salvation," that they can benefit fully from the means of salvation," (Vatican 2, Decree on Ecumenism, 3).

CCC 2068, "so that all men may attain salvation through faith, Baptism and the observance of the Commandments,"

Ephesians 1:13-14 <u>And you also were included in Christ when you heard the message of truth, the gospel of your salvation</u>. When you believed, you were marked in him with a seal, the promised Holy Spirit, [14] who is a deposit guaranteeing our inheritance until the redemption of those who are God's possession—to the praise of his glory

Ephesians 2:8-9 For it is by grace you have been saved, through faith and this is not from yourselves, <u>it is the gift of God— 9 not by works</u> so that no one can boast

2:10 For we are God's handiwork, created in Christ Jesus to do good works, which God prepared in advance for us to do

2 Timothy 1:9 <u>He has saved us</u> and called us to a holy life, not because of anything we have done but because of his own purpose and grace. This grace was given us in Christ Jesus before the beginning of time

8. **The Eucharist** given in the mass <u>goes completely against what Scripture teaches us below</u>

The Catholic Church says that the bread and wine literally become the blood and body of Christ when taken as communion (the Eucharist). Communion is the verb-being a part of Communion or being in Communion with the saints. The Eucharist is the noun, meaning the person of Jesus Christ.

Some of the churches that believe in this so-called miracle include; the Catholic Church, Eastern Orthodox, Oriental Orthodox, Anglican, Presbyterian, and Lutheran churches.

The miracles performed in the Bible showed a drastic change in appearance. The Eucharistic host doesn't.

CCC 1374, "…In the most blessed sacrament of the Eucharist "<u>the body and blood, together with the soul and divinity, of our Lord Jesus Christ and</u>, **<u>therefore, the whole Christ is truly, really, and substantially contained</u>**."

CCC 1376, "The Council of Trent summarizes the Catholic faith by declaring: "Because Christ our Redeemer said that it was truly his body that he was offering under the species of bread, it has always been the conviction of the Church of God, and this holy Council now declares again, <u>that by the consecration of the bread and wine there takes place a change of the whole substance of the bread into the substance of the body of Christ our Lord and of the whole substance of the wine into the substance of his blood</u>. This change the holy Catholic Church has fittingly and properly called transubstantiation."

Hebrews 9:28 – <u>So, Christ was sacrificed once</u> to take away the sins of many; and he will appear a second time, not to bear sin, but to bring salvation to those who are waiting for him

Again, Christ was sacrificed once and only once

Matthew 24:27-30 - For as lightning that comes from the east is visible even in the west, so will be the coming of the Son of Man…

The Scripture above and the two below, show that Jesus is physically in Heaven, as discussed in Chapter 3, and will not return to earth physically until his Second Coming.

Acts 1:11 - Men of Galilee, they said, "Why do you stand here looking into the sky? This same Jesus, who has been taken from you into heaven, **will come back in the same way you have seen him go into heaven**."

Hebrews 10:12 - <u>But when this priest</u> had offered <u>for all time one sacrifice for sins</u>, he sat down at the right hand of God.

Offered once and is in Heaven physically.

Hebrews 8:13 - By calling this covenant "new," he has made the first one obsolete; and what is obsolete and outdated will soon disappear.

This means that the priesthood and other practices were done away with.

Leviticus 17:12 – Therefore, I say to the Israelites, "None of you may eat blood, nor may any foreigner residing among you eat blood.

The Catholic Church claims you eat Jesus' blood with the Eucharist; a violation of the above Scripture.

With Jesus' sacrifice for us, the Priesthood ended and Jesus became the High Priest. Those churches that say Jesus comes down thousands of times each day in the Eucharist are insulting Jesus and fooling millions. Thousands of times each day they make Jesus a victim. How ridiculous that a Priest (an ordinary sinful man), can say they have the power to physically bring Jesus down from Heaven each time they have a mass!

Jesus said I am the one time sacrifice;

Hebrews 9:12 - He did not enter by means of the blood of goats and calves; but he entered the Most Holy Place once for all by his own blood, thus, obtaining eternal redemption

Hebrews 26 - Otherwise Christ would have had to suffer many times since the creation of the world. But he has appeared once for all at the culmination of the ages to do away with sin by the sacrifice of himself.

9.   **Penance and Indulgences** is necessary for salvation.

Penance and selling of indulgences, led to the Protestant Reformation of 1517. This was the time numerous members left the Catholic Church. Penance is an act of devotion, where the person performs prayers, charitable work, etc., to show sorrow or repentance.

CCC 980, "This sacrament of Penance is necessary for salvation for those who have fallen after Baptism, just as Baptism is necessary for salvation for those who have not yet been reborn."

10. **Indulgences are** defined by the Catholic Church as the granting of full or partial remission of the punishment of sin.

This means, for cash you can have sins taken away-for you, you're family, or even your departed loved ones.

CCC 1471, "The doctrine and practice of indulgences in the Church are closely linked to the effects of the sacrament of Penance. What is an indulgence? 'An indulgence is a remission before God of the temporal punishment due to sins whose guilt has already been forgiven, which the faithful Christian who is duly disposed gains under certain prescribed conditions through the action of the Church which, as the minister of redemption, dispenses and applies with authority the treasury of the satisfactions of Christ and the saints.' 'An indulgence is partial or plenary according, as it removes either part or all of the temporal punishment due to sin.' The faithful can gain indulgences for themselves or apply them to the dead."

CCC 1478, "An indulgence is obtained through the Church who, by virtue of the power of binding and loosing granted her by Christ Jesus, intervenes in favor of individual Christians and opens for them the treasury of the merits of Christ and the saints to obtain from the Father of mercies the remission of the temporal punishments due for their sins. Thus, the Church does not want simply to come to the aid of these Christians, but also to spur them to works of devotion, penance, and charity.

CCC 1498, "Through indulgences, the faithful can obtain the remission of temporal punishment, resulting from sin for themselves and also for the souls in Purgatory."

Indulgence is the payment of money for full or partial forgiveness of sins, for a living or a dead person. The St. Peters Basilica was built with indulgence payments, so were hospitals, churches, schools, etc. Those paying masses for their dead loved ones (indulgences), according to the Scripture below, are wasting their money.

Hebrews 9:27 clearly notes, "**Just as people are destined to die once, and after that to face judgment**".

1 Peter 1:18-19 - For you know that it was not with perishable things, **such as silver or gold, that you were redeemed** from the empty way of life handed down to you from your ancestors, [19] but with the precious blood of Christ, a lamb without blemish or defect.

Galatians 1:6-9 - <u>I am astonished that you are so quickly deserting the one who called you to live in the grace of Christ, and are turning to a different gospel 7 which is really no gospel at all</u>. Evidently, some people are throwing you into confusion and are trying to pervert the gospel of Christ. [8] But even if we or an angel from heaven should preach a gospel other than the one we preached to you, let them be under God's curse! [9] As we have already said, so now I say again: **If anybody is preaching to you a gospel other than what you accepted, let them be under God's curse!**

Psalms 49:6-9 those who trust in their wealth and boast of their great riches? [7] No one can redeem the life of another or give to God a ransom for them; [8] the ransom for a life is costly; no payment is ever enough, [9] so they should live on forever and not see decay.

11. **Veneration of Mary and her statutes**

1 John 2:1 - My dear children, I write this to you so that you will not sin. But if anybody does sin, we have an advocate with the Father Jesus Christ, the Righteous One.

1 Timothy 2:5 - For there is one God and <u>one mediator between God and mankind, the man Christ Jesus.</u>

Psalms 135:15-18 - The idols of the nations are silver and gold, made by human hands. [16] <u>They have mouths, but cannot speak, eyes, but cannot see.</u> [17] <u>They have ears, but cannot hear</u>, nor is there breath in their mouths. [18] Those who make them will be like them, and so will all who trust in them.

Exodus 20:3-6 - <u>You shall not make for yourself an image in the form of anything in heaven above or on the earth beneath or in the waters below.</u> [5] <u>You shall not bow down to them or worship them</u>; for I, the Lord your God, am a jealous God, punishing the children for the sin of the parents to the third and fourth generation of those who hate me, [6] but showing love to a thousand generations of those who love me and keep my commandments.

12. **The use of holy water and the rosary**

No earthly (formed or not formed) object has power and should not be used in praying.

2 Kings 18:4 He removed the high places, smashed the sacred stones, and cut down the Asherah poles. He broke into pieces the bronze snake Moses had made, for up to that time the Israelites had been burning incense to it.

Exodus 23:24 - Do not bow down before their gods or worship them or follow their practices. You must demolish them and break their sacred stones to pieces.

13. **Canonization of dead saints**

Throughout the New Testament saints **are living Christians**, not people who have died. The NIV Bible calls them "Holy People" other Bibles call them Saints.

2 Corinthians 1:1 - Paul, an apostle of Christ Jesus by the will of God, and Timothy our brother, To the church of God in Corinth, together with all his holy people throughout Achaia.

Ephesians 1:1 - Paul, an apostle of Christ Jesus by the will of God, To God's holy people in Ephesus, the faithful in Christ Jesus.

Romans 1:7 - To all those in Rome who are loved by God and called to be saints: Grace to you and peace from God our Father and the Lord Jesus Christ (English Standard Version).

Acts 9:13 - But Ananias answered, "Lord, I have heard from many about this man, how much evil he has done to your saints at Jerusalem (English Standard Version).

14. **Celibacy of the priesthood** (an oath not to marry or have sex).

1 Timothy 3:2-5 - Now, the overseer is to be above reproach, faithful to his wife, temperate, self-controlled, respectable, hospitable, able to teach, [3] not given to drunkenness, not violent but gentle, not quarrelsome, not

a lover of money. [4] He must manage his own family well and see that his children obey him, and he must do so in a manner worthy of full respect. [5] If anyone does not know how to manage his own family, how can he take care of God's church?

15. **Following Tradition also called Man-made rules leads to perversion** (to cause one to turn away from what is morally true and right).

It was not until 1546, at the Council of Trent, that the Roman Catholic Church declared for the first time its official position that the gospel is contained in both Scripture and Tradition.

Additional manmade customs include the concepts of the monks, nuns, monasteries, convents, 40 day Lent, Holy Week, Ash Wednesday, and All Saints Day.

All of the above celebrations and concepts are not found in the Bible. In fact, the Monastery concept goes completely against the idea of Christians coming together.

Mark 7:6-9 - He replied, "Isaiah was right when he prophesied about you hypocrites; as it is written:

"'These people honor me with their lips, but their hearts are far from me. [7] They worship me in vain; their teachings are merely human rules.' [8] You have let go of the commands of God and are holding on to human traditions." [9] And he continued, "You have a fine way of setting aside the commands of God in order to observe your own traditions!'"

CCC 81 "And [Holy] *Tradition* transmits in its entirety the Word of God which has been entrusted to the apostles by Christ the Lord and the Holy Spirit. It transmits it to the successors of the apostles, so that, enlightened by the Spirit of truth, they may faithfully preserve, expound and spread it abroad by their preaching."

CCC 82, "…the Church, to whom the transmission and interpretation of Revelation is entrusted, **does not derive her certainty about all revealed truths from the Holy Scriptures alone. Both Scripture and**

Tradition must be accepted and honored with equal sentiments of devotion and reverence."

Tradition in the Catholic Church says that when traditions and their declarations conflict with Scripture, tradition and declarations prevail (win).

CCC 100, "The task of interpreting the Word of God authentically has been entrusted solely to the Magisterium [the teaching authority] of the Church, that is, to the Pope and to the bishops in communion with him."

Isaiah 29:13 - These people come near to me with their mouth and honor me with their lips, but their hearts are far from me. <u>Their worship of me is made up only of rules taught by man.</u>

Deuteronomy 4:2 - <u>Do not add to what I command you and do not subtract from it,</u> but keep the commands of the Lord your God that I give you.

Deuteronomy 12:29-32 - The Lord your God will cut off before you the nations you are about to invade and dispossess. But when you have driven them out and settled in their land, [30] and after they have been destroyed before you, be careful not to be ensnared by inquiring about their gods, saying, "How do these nations serve their gods? We will do the same." [31] <u>You must not worship the Lord your God in their way,</u> because in worshiping their gods, they do all kinds of detestable things the Lord hates. They even burn their sons and daughters in the fire as sacrifices to their gods.

Matthew 15:8 - These people honor me with their lips, but their hearts are far from me.[9] They worship me in vain; <u>their teachings are merely human rules.</u>

John 15:4 - See to it that no one takes you captive through hollow and deceptive philosophy, <u>which depends on human tradition</u> and the elemental spiritual forces of this world, rather than on Christ.

Acts 17:11 – Now, the Berean Jews were of more noble character than those in Thessalonica, for they received the message with great eagerness and examined the Scriptures every day to see if what Paul said was true.

Psalms 118:9 - It is better to take refuge in the Lord than to trust in princes.

Psalms 146:3 - Do not put your trust in princes, in human beings, who cannot save.

Jeremiah 17:5 - Cursed is the one who trusts in man, who draws strength from mere flesh and whose heart turns away from the Lord.

Galatians 1:10 - Am I now trying to win the approval of human beings, or of God? Or am I trying to please people? If I were still trying to please people, I would not be a servant of Christ.

1 Corinthians 15:1-3 - Now, brothers and sisters, I want to remind you of the gospel I preached to you, which you received and on which you have taken your stand. ² By this gospel, you are saved, if you hold firmly to the word I preached to you. Otherwise, you have believed in vain.

More on human Tradition-Peter 1:17-19, 2 Thessalonians 2:10-11, Acts 17:11, 1 Corinthians 15:1-4, Jeremiah 17:5-8, Proverbs 3:5-6, 28:26, 30:5-6, Psalms 118:8-9,146:3 and Isaiah 2:22.

16. Infallibility

The meaning of infallibility is that the Pope cannot err when he teaches in matters of faith and morals.

The Catholic Church bases all of its infallible teachings on supposedly sacred tradition and sacred scripture.

In 1870, at the First Vatican Council, Pope Pius the Ninth declared in the doctrine of Papal Infallibility; that the Pope possessed full and complete power and authority over the whole church, that the Pope can rule independently of any matter which comes under its sphere of the church's jurisdiction, without the concurrence of the bishops or the rest of the church and that there is no higher authority on earth than the Pope.

CCC 2035, "The supreme degree of participation in the authority of Christ is ensured by the charism of infallibility. This infallibility extends as far as does the deposit of divine Revelation; it also extends to all those elements of doctrine, including morals, without which the saving truths of the faith cannot be preserved, explained, or observed."

It is with degrees and dogmas (a set of principles) that has become the final authority of the Roman Catholic Church.

John 14:6 - Jesus answered, "I am the way and the truth and the life. No one comes to the Father except through me."

John 17:3 – Now, this is eternal life: that they know you, the only true God, and Jesus Christ, whom you have sent.

17. **Baptism in the Catholic Church** includes an exorcism on its members, and the priest <u>forgives the one being baptized of all their sins, and that, once baptized, the baby or others are Born Again</u>.

CCC 1263, "By baptism all sins are forgiven, original sin and all personal sins, as well as all punishment for sin..."

The above CCC paragraph contradicts the Catholic Churches concept of Purgatory.

Exorcism;

CCC 1237, "Since Baptism signifies liberation from sin and from its instigator the devil, **one or more exorcisms are pronounced over the candidate...**"

In the Bible, all exorcisms were performed on people possessed by the Devil or his agents.

As discussed in the Born Again chapter, one must repent of their sins, which leads to being Born Again, which leads to receiving the Holy Spirit, and finally, you get baptized. How can a baby repent?

The Catholic Church should change its name to "The Church of Mary and the Saints" since that is who they worship and pray to.

The supposed successors to Peter Who were absolutely nothing like Peter

Pope Sergius III, 904 to 911:

- He reputedly ordered the murder of his two immediate predecessors, Pope Leo V and the anti-pope Christopher. Pope Leo was apparently strangled under Sergius' orders.

- Sergius considered Pope John IX, Pope Benedict IV, and Leo V antipopes.

- He was reputed by several sources, to have been the lover of Marozia. Both Marozia and her sister Theodora were prostitutes.

- Marozia's family included an illegitimate son, two grandsons, and one great grandson-all who became popes

- Pope John XIII was her nephew from her sister Theodora.

- Sergius' reign began a period known as "the rule of the harlots".

- He promoted family members in the church

Pope John XII, 955 to 964:

- He was the son of Duke Alberic II, the ruler of Rome. He became pope at about the age of 18 years-old

- Pope John was known as a robber, murderer, and incestuous person who enjoyed drinking and gambling.

- John was an immoral man. The bishop of Cremona, Luitprand said, "No honest lady dared to show herself in public, for Pope John had no respect either for single girls, married women, or widows – they were sure to be defiled by him …"

Pope Boniface VIII, 1294 to 1303:

- He lived off of stolen money.

- Boniface was quoted saying, "To enjoy oneself and lie carnally with women or with boys is no more a sin than rubbing one's hands together."

Pope John XXII, 1316 to 1334:

- John was said to have seduced and violated three hundred nuns. He kept a harem of no less than two hundred girls. He was called "the most depraved criminal who ever sat on the papal throne."

- A Vatican record says this about him, "His lordship, Pope John, committed perversity with the wife of his brother, incest with holy nuns, intercourse with virgins, adultery with the married, and all sorts of sex crimes...wholly given to sleep and other carnal desires, totally adverse to the life and teaching of Christ...he was publicly called the Devil incarnate."

Pope Pius II, 1464 to 1471:

- Pius was said to have been the father of many illegitimate children. He spoke openly of the methods he used to seduce women, and he encouraged young men to also seduce women, and even offered to instruct them in methods of self-indulgence.

Pope Sixtus IV, 1471 to 1484:

- He financed his wars by selling church offices to the highest bidders. He used the papacy to enrich himself and his family.

- No less than eight cardinals were his nephews, some being given the position of cardinal as young boys.

Pope Alexander VI, 1492 to 1503:

- He won the election of the papacy by bribery. He was made a cardinal by his uncle who was Pope Calixtus III -He lived with a woman with whom he had a daughter; whom afterward he committed incest with and produced one, some sources say five, children.

- <u>He also lived in public incest with his sister and produced a child</u> and had six illegitimate children.

- He made six of his nephews cardinals.

- He conducted a sex orgy in the Vatican in which he had a banquet featuring fifty nude girls who danced and serviced the guests – and even offered prizes to the man who could engage in sexual intercourse the most times.

All the bishops and popes since the Catholic Churches beginning (313 A.D.) have not had the courage to put the Catholic Church in line with the Word of God (the Bible).

Revelation 18:4 - Come out of her, my people, so that you will not share in her sins, so that you will not receive any of her plagues.

Martin Luther himself also witnessed that Rome, with its popes, was anything but a holy city. He was quoted as saying, "No one can imagine what sins and infamous actions are committed in Rome, they must be seen and heard to be believed." It has been said, "If there is a hell, Rome is built over it."

In the book "Dilemma, A Priest's Struggle with Faith and Love", 2011, former priest Albert Cutie says, "What makes this rule [celibacy] even more impossibly hypocritical is that the very office in Rome that issued that document is staffed by some of the most flamboyantly homosexual clergies."

The Roman Catholic Church under the Emperor Constantine:

Emperor Constantine, in a dream, was told to take the Christian symbol into the Battle of the Milvian Bridge against Emperor Maxentius. On October 28, 312 A.D. Constantine ordered his troops to mark their shield with the symbol of 'Chi Rho', which was a representation of a long "P" with an "X" across the middle. This symbol represented the crucifixion of Jesus and his resurrection. On the way to battle, Constantine and his army witnessed a bright cross in the sky with the words "By this sign, Conquer", which they did.

In February 313 A.D., Constantine issued the Edict of Milan, which proclaimed Christianity and other religions legal. Before this time, Christians were being persecuted. Constantine then ordered the building of Christian churches and pagan temples simultaneously. Christianity then became the dominant religion over the pagan religions. During this time, was the birth of the Catholic Church, which was known as the Universal Church.

Conflicts began to rise between the pagan members and the Catholic Church. Pagan worshipers wanted the Catholics to allow their pagan rituals into their religion. The Catholic Church then began to incorporate, according to some historians, pagan rituals, maybe to increase their membership, and to satisfy the Emperor and the pagan worshipers. Saints replaced the cult of pagan gods, and mother and son pagan statutes were renamed 'Mary' and 'Jesus'.

In 431 A.D., Mary worship became the official doctrine of the Catholic Church, which renamed her "Christ-bearer" at the Council of Ephesus in July 431 A.D., at the church of Mary in Ephesus, in Anatolia.

The Roman emperors bore as heads of the pagan priesthood – *Pontifex Maximus* (Supreme Priest), and were worshipped by the pagans as gods. In 382, Emperor Gratian renounced the title and transferred it to the Bishop of Rome and ultimately went to the newly created position of pope. The popes also inherited Constantine's titles as the self-appointed civil head of the church – *Summus Pontifex* (Vicar of Christ and Bishop of Bishops). Just by the transfer of these titles, one can see Emperor Constantine was the Catholic Church's first pope.

Lastly, the abuse by the clergy and their staff members against young, innocent, children, and the cover-up of these abuses by leaders of the church, should have been the last straw; the awakening to leave this false religion. The total abuses, as of early 2022, are estimated at 17,000 abused children in the United States alone. This figure does not include the ones who didn't file complaints and the ones who have died over the many years of abuse. So far, the church has paid out over 3 billion dollars, and that is only in the United States.

Rape, especially of a child is so serious, that it creates a hole in one's soul. It's so shameful that the young children victims often prevent the full expression of their feelings for years.

I have a friend whose brother came from another town in New Mexico to live with him. His brother had a lot of emotional problems. My friend told me that his brother was an altar boy, and one day he came home crying and had blood coming out of his buttocks. Many of his family members witnessed this incident. The parents told the crying little boy and the other family members to never mention this to anyone and that it should stay in the family. At this critical time, the boy needed the support of his parents but got none. In those days, a priest was seen like he was God; many priests were never questioned or reported for their sinful behavior.

In 1906, a grand cousin of mine became the Justice of the Peace in Pecos, New Mexico. He started marrying the natives in his capacity as a judge. One Sunday, he went to church and sat in the first pew, my family sat in pew number ten. You sat in a specified pew according to your contributions to the Catholic Church. My relative, the judge, was the richest person in town, so, he sat in pew number one. The priest that Sunday, for his sermon, said, "There's someone going around town and marrying the natives. This is a sin and only a Catholic priest is authorized by God to marry a couple, and this person is going to go to hell." Hearing this, the judge fainted in his seat and had to be carried out by others. The next day, he traveled to Las Vegas, New Mexico, and resigned as Justice of the Peace. He didn't want to go to hell, because back then people saw and took the word of a priest, like if he was God.

Fourteen years ago, my brother, a Catholic died. On this rare occasion, I attended the funeral mass with my family. The priest and my brother knew each other well. The priest spoke very highly of my brother; and mentioned in church all the good he did for others and added, "Now you can pray to him," mentioning my brother's name, "and he will help you with your needs." I was ashamed for my brother for what the priest had said. We are required by Scripture, to go all the way up to the top <u>and pray to God only, through Jesus Christ</u>.

Many Catholics will say "I'm not a Christian I'm a Catholic", not knowing that one who believes in Jesus is a Christian. They'll also say, "I was born a Catholic and will die a Catholic", and "My family has been Catholics for centuries and I'll follow them." Have you ever heard a Catholic priest encouraging its members to read the Bible? I've heard them say it's too difficult to understand, <u>thus, keeping them from knowing the Truth</u> and receiving blessings as it says in the book of Revelation.

If only a Catholic would read the Bible, they would see that their opportunity for Everlasting Life is at stake, because God hates idol worshiping.

2 Corinthians 6:14-16 - Do not be yoked together with unbelievers. For what do righteousness and wickedness have in common? Or what fellowship can light have with darkness? ¹⁵ What harmony is there between Christ and Belial? Or what does a believer have in common with an unbeliever? ¹⁶ <u>What agreement is there between the temple of God and idols</u>? For we are the temple of the living God.

Isaiah 40:18 - With whom, then, will you compare God? To what image will you liken him?

Psalms 97:10 - Let those who love the Lord hate evil, for he guards the lives of his faithful ones and delivers them from the hand of the wicked.

Revelation 18:4-5 - Then I heard another voice from heaven say, "Come out of her, my people, so that you will not share in her sins, so that you will not receive any of her plagues; ⁵ for her sins are piled up to heaven, and God has remembered her crimes."

A good book on the Catholic Church is "Preparing for Eternity", by Mike Gendron.

Mormonism: The Church of Jesus Christ of Latter-day Saints

It is today's most seductive, non-Christian religion.

Galatians 1:6-9 - I am astonished that you are so quickly deserting the one who called you to live in the grace of Christ, and are turning to a different gospel, [7] which is really no gospel at all. Evidently, some people are throwing you into confusion and are trying to pervert the gospel of Christ. [8] But even if we or an angel from heaven should preach a gospel other than the one we preached to you, let them be under God's curse! [9] As we have already said, so now I say again: If anybody is preaching to you a gospel other than what you accepted, let them be under God's curse!

Apostle Paul uses the strongest possible Greek term, anathema, which means under the divine curse. To emphasize his point, he repeats it again in verse 9.

Here is the Mormons central theological axiom, called the Law of Eternal Progression:

- A man is, God once was, and as God is, man may become.

- Mormonism teaches that trillions of planets scattered throughout the cosmos are ruled by countless gods who once were human.

The Mormon Jesus:

To the Mormons, Jesus was their elder brother who pointed the way.

Jesus was the god of the Old Testament, but once he took his physical form, he had to justify or earn his own spiritual salvation through his works, while in the flesh. You will never see a cross in a Mormon church.

Jesus is the LDS savior, only in the sense that his death gives the Mormon the means, of returning to the god of this world, using the secret keys, handgrips, and passwords learned only in the Mormon Temple, secrets that will ensure safe passage through the doorway to personal godhead.

Proverbs 14:12 - There is a way that appears to be right, but in the end, it leads to death.

The Mormon God:

First; God the Father has a body of flesh and bone as tangible as Man's.

Second; God evolved from mortal man, all the way to man-God. In heaven, he has a body of flesh and bones.

Third; Mormons teach polytheism. Polytheism is the belief in the existence of more than one god. Mormons believe there are literally millions of gods; father gods, mother gods, grandfather gods, grandmother gods, even great uncles and aunts-literally millions of gods.

John 4:22-24 - You Samaritans worship what you do not know; we worship what we do know, for salvation is from the Jews. [23] Yet a time is coming and has now come when the true worshipers will worship the Father in the Spirit and in truth, for they are the kind of worshipers the Father seeks. [24] God is spirit, and his worshipers must worship in the Spirit and in truth.

One should test these beliefs against the teachings of God's Word. If God, Himself, doesn't know of any other gods, how could the Mormons know of millions of gods?

Isaiah 45:5-6 - "I am the Lord, and there is no other; apart from me, there is no God. I will strengthen you, though you have not acknowledged me, [6] so that from the rising of the sun to the place of its setting people may know there is none besides me. I am the Lord, and there is no other. Woe to those who quarrel with their Maker, those who are nothing but potsherds among the potsherds on the ground. Does the clay say to the potter, 'What are you making?' Does your work say, 'The potter has no hands'?"

Isaiah 45:21-22 - Declares what is to be; present it- let them take counsel together. Who foretold this long ago, who declared it from the distant past? Was it not I, the Lord? And there is no God apart from me, a righteous God and a Savior; there is none but me. ²² "Turn to me and be saved, all you ends of the earth; for I am God, and there is no other.

Mormonism believes in polytheism, and Christianity believes in Monotheism. In fact, it was because of the belief in polytheism that God destroyed the nations around Israel, and it was for following polytheism that God had Israel almost destroyed and sent into exile in 722 BC. It was for polytheism that God almost destroyed Judah in 586 BC and sent them into exile. God according to his Word absolutely condemns polytheism.

Michael Quinn, former professor of history at Brigham Young, wrote a book entitled "Early Mormonism in the Magic World View". In his book, he clearly documents the fact that Joseph Smith was heavily involved in the occult before he even began to receive revelations from his messengers of light.

2 Corinthians 11:4 - For if someone comes to you and preaches a Jesus other than the Jesus we preached, or if you receive a different spirit from the Spirit you received, or a different gospel from the one you accepted, you put up with it easily enough.

2 Corinthians 13:5 - Examine yourselves to see whether you are in the faith; test yourselves. Do you not realize that Christ Jesus is in you—unless, of course, you fail the test?

The LSD has never produced an official list of Smith's prophecies. Why? Maybe because of the 65 to 70 prophecies that were recorded, only 5 or 6 actually came to pass. That's a very poor record even for the worst of prophets.

Deuteronomy 18:20-22 - But a prophet who presumes to speak in my name anything I have not commanded, or a prophet who speaks in the name of other gods, is to be put to death.

²¹ You may say to yourselves, "How can we know when a message has not been spoken by the Lord?" ²² If what a prophet proclaims in the name of the Lord does not take place or come true, that is a message the Lord

has not spoken. That prophet has spoken presumptuously, so do not be alarmed.

The false teachings of the Jehovah Witnesses

Who is Jesus of the organization of Jehovah's Witnesses? It's the Archangel Michael. He was the first creation of God, he came to earth as a man, he died on a stake, and he rose invisibly as a ghost.

The Watch Tower Society was founded by Charles T. Russell. He said that he didn't like the teaching of hell, eternal judgment, or the teaching of the trinity. To him the trinity wasn't rational and he could not understand it. In 1884, the organization was incorporated in Pennsylvania, as the Watch Tower Bible and Tract Society.

Early in Russell's ministry, he calculated/prophesized when Jesus Christ was going to return visibly to this earth. He prophesied that Christ would return in 1874. When Christ didn't show up, he changed his calculations to 1914. When Christ didn't show up again, he redefined the second coming to mean that Christ would return as an invisible spirit-and Christ would help set up the organization. Russell died in 1916, having been proven a false prophet.

Judge Joseph Franklin Rutherford was the second leader of the organization. Under his leadership, the organization blossomed. His theocratic government believes they are God's government on earth and that all other governments are satanic. In the early 1920's Rutherford said (prophesized) that Abraham, Isaac, and Jacob would be resurrected in 1925 and would be the visible representatives of their organization here on earth. So, the Judge as he was called had a mansion in California built with money donated by its members. When the prophets did not show up, he moved his family into the mansion and lived there, until his death in 1942.

The Jehovah Witnesses' will not salute the flag, recite the pledge of allegiance, and will never serve in the armed forces of any nation. They deny the incarnation of Jesus Christ, that the true name of God is Jehovah and Jesus Christ and the Holy Spirit are not God or part of God.

It was under Rutherford that the Russellites changed/adopted the name Jehovah's Witnesses in 1931, partly to distinguish the Judges group from the splinter group that arose after Russell's death.

In ancient Hebrew, Jews did not use vowels, only consonants. They spelled God's name YHWH, the unutterable name used by the Jews. Most likely, it would have been pronounced "YAHWEH". Yahweh was anglicized as Jehovah many years ago; this name is not found in the manuscripts.

In 1942, Nathan H. Knorr took the leadership, and a strong missionary outreach was developed all over the world, and the printing of their translation of the Bible, which they call the New World Translation commenced. The Jehovah Witnesses claim that five of their scholars translated the Bible, **none of them had a background in the original Greek language**. It was quite obvious to Christian Theologians that there were gross errors. Their Bible was translated to meet their conceived Witness theology.

Five important facts about Jehovah Witnesses:

1. Their Organization is the prophet of God.

2. They are the sole channel for his Truth.

3. To reject the organization is to reject God.

4. They believe that the Watch Tower Magazine contains God's truth.

5. Only the Organization can interpret the Bible.

Conflicts with Christianity:

1. Jesus is a created being-a creature.

2. Jesus is Michael the Archangel.

3. Jesus <u>was not resurrected bodily</u>, but as a spiritual being.

4. Jesus returned invisibly in 1914 (secretly to the organization).

5. Jesus was only a man when on earth, not the "Word became flesh."

6. The Holy Spirit is only God's active force, not the Person of God.

7. Hell is simply the grave.

8. That Heaven's doors are open to only 144,000 people and they select those individuals. Under their first leader Russell, only 144,000 were going to be saved and would reside in Heaven. Since the organization grew, they had to change their belief, so now; the rest of the Witnesses will remain on earth.

9. Salvation is found only through the organization.

10. Satan is the author of the trinity.

11. And that Jesus cannot be given worship, but only honor as Jehovah's creation.

Some of the many Biblical Scriptures that conflict with what Jehovah Witnesses' believe:

Zechariah 12:1 - The Lord, who stretches out the heavens, who lays the foundation of the earth, and who forms the human spirit within a person, declares:

12:10 - And I will pour out on the house of David and the inhabitants of Jerusalem a spirit of grace and supplication. <u>They will look on me, the one they have pierced, and they will mourn for him as one mourns for an only child</u>, and grieve bitterly for him as one grieves for a firstborn son.

John 20:28 - Thomas said to him [Jesus], <u>"My Lord and my God!"</u>

Colossians 2:9 - <u>For in Christ all the fullness of the Deity lives in bodily form.</u>

Matthew 2:10-12 - When they saw the star, they were overjoyed. On coming to the house, they saw the child with his mother Mary, <u>and they</u>

bowed down and worshiped him. Then they opened their treasures and presented him with gifts of gold, frankincense, and myrrh. And having been warned in a dream not to go back to Herod, they returned to their country by another route.

28:19 – Therefore, go and make disciples of all nations, baptizing them in the name of the Father and of the Son and of the Holy Spirit.

Acts 13:2 - While they were worshiping the Lord and fasting, the Holy Spirit said, "Set apart for me Barnabas and Saul for the work, to which I have called them."

Revelation 22:18-19 - I warn everyone who hears the words of the prophecy of this book**: If anyone adds to them, God will add to him the plagues described in this book,** and if anyone takes away from the words of the book of this prophecy, God will take away his share in the tree of life and in the holy city, which are described in this book.

Proverbs 30:5-6 - Every word of God proves true; he is a shield to those who take refuge in him. **Do not add to his words, lest He rebuke you and you be found a liar.**

Never allow a Jehovah's Witness to read his or her bible; it's very perverted (corrupted and distorted), from the True Bible. The Jehovah Witnesses wrote their bible to fit their fairy tale. Read your Bible to them.

- -

All that you have read about from the different false religions does not correspond with Scripture. In fact, it is an insult to Scripture "The Truth", to God and Jesus.

The false Christian religions you've read about; teach a completely different God, Jesus, Mary, and Saints than the True Bible.

A Mormon will talk to you more about Joseph Smith than Jesus Christ. A Catholic will talk to you more about man-made rules/traditions than Scripture.

The most important thing I can tell you is, don't trust man, trust what's in the Bible for Everlasting Life.

So-called churches that allow gays or lesbians as teachers or pastors against the wishes of the Bible:

The Metropolitan Community, United Church of Christ, Evangelical Lutheran Church in America, Presbyterian Church (USA), Episcopal in the United States, Christian Church (Disciples of Christ), and the Old Catholic Church.

So-called churches that allow women to be in leading roles (like Bishops) and head of the clergy:

Episcopal Church, American Baptist Church, Evangelical Lutheran Church in America, Presbyterian Church USA, United Methodist Church, Unitarian Universalist, and United Church of Christ.

1 Corinthians 14:34 - Women should remain silent in the churches. They are not allowed to speak, but must be in submission, as the law says.

1 Timothy 2:12 - I do not permit a woman to teach or to assume authority over a man; she must be quiet.

In Deuteronomy 6:14-15, God says: Do not follow other gods, the gods of the peoples around you, for the Lord your God, who is among you, is a jealous God and his anger will burn against you, and he will destroy you from the face of the land.

For those Christian religions that are lukewarm;

Revelation 3:15-16 - [Jesus speaking] "I know your deeds, that you are neither cold nor hot. I wish you were either one or the other! 16 So, because you are lukewarm, neither hot nor cold, I am about to spit you out of my mouth."

Romans 1:18-20 - The wrath of God is being revealed from heaven against all the godlessness and wickedness of people, who suppress the truth by their wickedness, [19] since what may be known about God is plain to them, because God has made it plain to them. [20] <u>For, since the creation of the world, God's invisible qualities; his eternal power and divine nature, have been clearly seen, being understood from what has been made, so that people are without excuse</u>.

For the false religions mentioned, and others not mentioned, they'll only guide you to eternity in Hell. Concern yourselves with living in everlasting life with God and Jesus.

In John 14:6 Jesus says "I am the way the <u>truth</u> and the life."

1 Corinthians 6:9-11 - Or do you not know that wrongdoers will not inherit the kingdom of God? Do not be deceived: Neither the sexually immoral nor idolaters nor adulterers nor men who have sex with men [10] nor thieves nor the greedy nor drunkards nor slanderers nor swindlers will inherit the kingdom of God. [11] And that is what some of you were. But you were washed, you were sanctified, you were justified in the name of the Lord Jesus Christ and by the Spirit of our God.

The Berean's were residents of the ancient city of Berea in Macedonia;

Acts 17:11 - Now the Berean Jews were of more noble character than those in Thessalonica, for they received the message with great eagerness and examined the Scriptures every day to see if what Paul said was true.

Everyone who hears someone preach should examine the Scriptures, like the Bereans did, to see if that person is telling the Truth that is in Scripture. Always remember, that any teachings or traditions that conflict with Scripture are under God's curse.

Galatians 1:8-9 - But even if we or an angel from heaven should preach a gospel other than the one we preached to you, let them be under God's curse! [9] As we have already said, so now I say again: If anybody is preaching to you a gospel other than what you accepted, let them be under God's curse!

False teachers are condemned not once but twice.

All those who are members of false religions have been deprived of knowing and having a relationship with the True God; yesterday, today, and forever. Their loss is worse than living in a world of fear, sickness, prejudice, and poverty.

Here's a view of one of God's creations. Imagine what the world looked like before the great flood

CHAPTER 7

BOASTING IN THE BIBLE

Many Reasons why we should not boast in ourselves or others:

People like to make others heroes or heroines, because of their service or action in a particular situation, task, or because of their talents. Governments and others name buildings after their own. In Santa Fe, you see parks, streets, statutes, buildings, and shopping centers named after individuals. Many of the state buildings in Santa Fe are named after politicians. Public and private schools name their schools, gymnasiums, and cafeterias after former outstanding teachers, administrators, athletes, coaches, and students.

In Mount Rushmore, carved into the mountain's granite, you can see the head busts of George Washington, Thomas Jefferson, Theodore Roosevelt, and Abraham Lincoln. Throughout the United States, there are landmarks of historical significance, honoring people and events. Almost every city in the world is honoring its own.

In the last few years, monuments and memorials of questionable leaders, like Confederate leaders, have been torn down across various states, because of their involvement in slavery and colonialism. Some of the Spanish heroes in the colonialism of the Southwest were murderers, and cared only about making a financial profit.

Supreme Court Justice Ruth Ginsberg voted on every decision in support of advancing LGBTQ rights and played a central role in defending abortion rights. The state of New York honored Ginsberg by placing a statute of her that you can see very clearly as you enter Brooklyn from the Manhattan Bridge. Other statutes of her are to come.

What happens to a living person when they make them a hero/heroin? For sure they believe they are above the average person, or that they accomplished something extraordinary. Shouldn't we be encouraging them to be thankful to God for what good they've done? Don't all good things including courage come from God above?

This hero recognition goes so far as religious leaders putting their names on the front cover of Bibles. You have the King James Bible and other Bibles which have the preacher's name on the front cover of the Holy Bible! The impression one gets is, did that person write it, or did they sign off to approve the contents of the Bible?

You have hotels, ski resorts, realtors, restaurants, and other businesses boasting-by displaying or advertising beautiful views of the mountains, the colorful ocean, and the breathtaking views of the night skies, without giving any credit to the Creator!

Newspapers are one of the biggest sources in making people heroes\ heroines; in the sports world in the business sector, in the school academics, with artists, musicians, etc. Museums are another organization that honors people of wars, cultures, and governments.

So-called prestigious awards; the Noble Prize (for various fields), Grammy Awards, Pulitzer Prize (accomplishments in journalism, literature, and music), the Triple Crown (for acting), Hilton Humanitarian Prize, Academy Awards, Golden Globe Awards, and on and on and on are honoring people, not God.

This idea of honoring others goes even further; people give credit to their family genes for the occupations and talents they have, rather than giving credit where credit was due, with the true God-the Creator, who gave them these talents.

In 2021, the government and others were calling the policemen and health workers heroes for staying on the job during the corona virus. At the beginning of 2022, they started to fire them because they refused to get the corona virus shot. Isn't this a contradiction?

If these heroes' and heroines' actions are in line with good deeds, bravery, or courage; who gave these people of honors this ability? As we'll see below it was God. People should be honoring and crediting God.

We shouldn't be making others; heroes, heroines, icons, or calling people stars, super stars, movie stars, famous and celebrity:

Jeremiah 9:22-24 - Let not the wise man boast about his riches.

1 Corinthians 15:9-11 - The Apostle Paul speaking about the other apostles, "For I am the least of the apostles, and do not even deserve to be called an apostle, because I persecuted the church of God. [10] But by the grace of God I am what I am, and his grace to me was not without effect. No, I worked harder than all of them—yet not I, but the grace of God that was with me. [11] Whether, then, it is I or they, this is what we preach, and this is what you believed."

2 Corinthians 12:1-7 - I must go on boasting. Although there is nothing to be gained, I will go on to visions and revelations from the Lord. [2] I know a man in Christ who fourteen years ago was caught up to the third heaven. Whether it was in the body or out of the body I do not know— God knows. [3] And I know that this man—whether in the body or apart from the body I do not know, but God knows— [4] was caught up to paradise and heard inexpressible things, things that no one is permitted to tell. [5] I will boast about a man like that, but I will not boast about myself, except about my weaknesses. [6] Even if I should choose to boast, I would not be a fool, because I would be speaking the truth. But I refrain, so no one will think more of me than is warranted by what I do or say, or because of these surpassingly great revelations. Therefore, in order to keep me from becoming conceited, I was given a thorn in my flesh, a messenger of Satan, to torment me.

God gave Paul a thorn in his flesh so he wouldn't boast.

2 Corinthians 11:16-17 - I repeat: Let no one take me for a fool. But if you do, then tolerate me just as you would a fool, so that I may do a little boasting. [17] <u>In this self-confident boasting I am not talking as the Lord would, but as a fool.</u>

1 Corinthians 3:18-23 - For the wisdom of the world is foolishness in God's sight.

Psalm 44:6-8 - [6] I put no trust in my bow, my sword does not bring me victory; [7] but you give us victory over our enemies, you put our adversaries to shame. [8] <u>In God we make our boast all day long, and we will praise your name forever.</u>

Proverbs 27:1-2 - Do not boast about tomorrow.

1 Corinthians 1:18-31 - Has not God made foolish the wisdom of the world?

2 Corinthians 11:30 - If I must boast, <u>I will boast of the things that show my weakness.</u>

1 Corinthians 1:31 - Therefore, as it is written: "<u>Let the one who boasts boast in the Lord.</u>"

Romans 12:3 - For by the grace given me I say to every one of you: **Do not think of yourself more highly than you ought**, but rather think of yourself with sober judgment, in accordance with the faith God has distributed to each of you.

Romans 4:2 - If, in fact, Abraham was justified by works, he had something to boast about—**but not before God.**

1 Corinthians 2:1 - And so it was with me, brothers and sisters. When I came to you, <u>I did not come with eloquence or human wisdom as I proclaimed to you the testimony about God.</u>

James 4:6 But he gives us more grace. That is why Scripture says: "<u>God opposes the proud but shows favor to the humble.</u>

Matthew 23:12 - For those who exalt themselves will be humbled, and those who humble themselves will be exalted.

Proverbs 11:2 - <u>When pride comes, then comes disgrace, but with humility comes wisdom</u>.

Galatians 1:10 - **Am I now trying to win the approval of human beings, or of God? Or am I trying to please people? If I were still trying to please people, I would not be a servant of Christ.**

Galatians 6:4 - Each one should test their own actions. <u>Then they can take pride in themselves alone, without comparing themselves to someone else.</u>

Matthew 20:25-26 - Jesus called them together and said, "You know that the rulers of the Gentiles lord it over them, and their high officials exercise authority over them. Not so with you. **Instead, whoever wants to become great among you, must be your servant.**

Matthew 18:4 - Therefore, whoever takes the lowly position of this child is the greatest in the kingdom of heaven.

1 Peter 5:6 - **Humble yourselves, therefore, under God's mighty hand, that he may lift you up in due time.**

Ephesians 2:8-9 - For it is by grace you have been saved, through faith, and this is not from yourselves, **it is the gift of God — not by works so that no one can boast**.

1 Corinthians 4:7 - For who makes you different from anyone else? <u>**What do you have that you did not receive? And if you did receive it, why do you boast as though you did not?**</u>

John 15:19 - Woe to you, who all men speak well of you.

The below Scripture tells us who are heroes, and what humans we should imitate and use as role-models:

Psalms 34:1-22 - David said, "My soul will boast in the Lord."

1 Corinthians 11:1 - Follow my example, as I follow the example of Christ.

Philippians 3:17 - <u>Join together in following my example, brothers and sisters, and just as you have us as a model</u>, keep your eyes on those who live as we do.

Hebrews 13:7 - Remember your leaders, who spoke the word of God to you. <u>Consider the outcome of their way of life and imitate their faith.</u>

1 John 2:16 - **For everything in the world**; the lust of the flesh, the lust of the eyes, **and the pride of life, comes not from the Father but from the world.**

The Bible says we should imitate or model the apostles. The Bible also says we were created to glorify God. When you glorify God you boast about Him.

The Scriptures in the Bible that use the word hero are used in a negative way, showing that mankind should not be considered heroes and heroines;

Genesis 6:4 - "The Nephilim were on the earth in those days—and also afterward—when the sons of God went to the daughters of humans and had children by them." They were the heroes of old, men of renown.

Above, is the main reason why God decided to wipe out man and animals, with the great flood of Noah's days. He was grieved that He had made man and God's heart was filled with pain, over the evilness of these so called heroes.

Psalms 52:1 - Why do you boast of evil, you mighty hero? Why do you boast all day long, <u>you who are a disgrace in the eyes of God</u>?

Isaiah 5:22 - "Woe to those who are heroes at drinking wine and champions at mixing drinks. <u>You acquit the guilty for a bribe, but deny justice to the innocent.</u>"

Boasting in yourself or others is like bragging, and both behaviors are rooted in pride and thus it's a sin. Boasting in yourself or others is idol worship.

CHAPTER 8

VARIOUS "TRUE CHRISTIAN" TOPICS

The only Sacrifices a True Christian would participate in;

1. Mark 10:45 - For even the Son of Man <u>did not come to be served, but to serve</u>, and to give his life as a ransom for many.

2. Ephesians 5:2 – And walk in the way of love, just as Christ loved us and gave himself up for us, <u>as a fragrant offering and sacrifice to God.</u>

3. Romans 12:1 - Therefore, I urge you, brothers and sisters, in view of God's mercy, to <u>offer your bodies as a living sacrifice, holy and pleasing to God—this is your true and proper worship.</u>

4. Luke 9:23 – Then, he said to them all: "Whoever wants to be my disciple <u>must deny themselves and take up their cross daily and follow me."</u>

5. Proverbs 21:3 - <u>To do what is right and just is more acceptable to the Lord than sacrifice.</u>

How many years ago was Man Created?

Genesis 1:27 So, <u>God created mankind in his own image</u>, in the image of God he created them; male and female he created them.

The universe and the earth are an unknown age.

The Jews, according to the Torah, say Man has been around for 5,783 years:

3761 B.C.
2022 A.D.
5,783 years

Scriptures that says there's Life after death

1. Psalms 116:5 - Precious in the sight of the Lord, is the death of his saints.

2. Mathew 22:32 - He is not the God of the dead, but the living.

3. Revelation 6:10 - They called out in a loud voice "how long" sovereign Lord, holy and true, until you judge the inhabitants of the earth and avenge our blood?

4. Mark 9:2 - The transfiguration of Jesus, Elijah, and Moses, witnessed by Peter, James, and John.

5. Luke 16:19 - The story of the Rich man and Lazarus is not a parable, parables do not use names.

6. Matthew 27:51 - At that moment the curtain of the temple was torn in two from top to bottom. The earth shook, the rocks split and the tombs broke open. The bodies of many holy people who had died were raised to life. They came out of the tombs after Jesus' resurrection and went into the holy city and appeared too many people.

7. 1 Corinthians 15:16 – **If the dead are not raised, then Christ has not been raised either.**

8. 1 Corinthians 15:20 - **Christ has indeed been raised from the dead, the first fruits of those who have fallen asleep.**

9. Philippians 1:23 - I am torn between the two: I desire to depart and be with Christ, which is better by far.

10. 1 Peter 4:6 - For this is the reason the gospel was preached even to those who are now dead, so that they might be judged according to human standards in regard to the body, but live according to God in regard to the spirit.

11. Luke 20:37 - in the account of the burning bush, even Moses showed that the dead rise; for he calls the Lord the God of Abraham, the God of Isaac, and the God of Jacob.

Something's a True Christian would say or do:

TC means True Christian.

1. If someone asked a True Christian to do something wrong, a TC would generally say, I won't sin against God. Most others would think first of the consequences for themselves and second the consequences for others.

2. A TC understands very well that their occupation was given to them by God, and will do their best to do a good job.

3. A TC believes first in the Scriptures, and all other teachings would have to support Scriptures' concepts.

4. Jesus said, "The world loves its own, but hates those whom He chose out of the world." - John 15:19 and

"Woe to you who all men speak well of you"-Luke 6:26.

A TC understands these two Scriptures.

5. A TC would never support; abortions, homosexual, and transgender behaviors, or proposed laws in those areas.

6. Many people would say my main goal in life is to make money, to pay my bills, to have money so my family can enjoy life, to be respected by others, to be liked by others, to get a good education, etc. A TC would say my main goal in life is to do what pleases God.

7. A TC is often praying for the poor, the innocent, the Jews, those not Saved, those in authority, and those having troubles in their lives.

8. A TC is ready to help others in need and those they have had differences with. They also know that their actions of helping a person they have had difficulty with in the past, is a great accomplishment-if they help lead them to Jesus.

Matthew 5:46 - If you love those who love you, what reward will you get? Are not even the tax collectors doing that?

9. Some people are obsessed with watching sports on TV, especially football, constantly concerned with exercising, perfecting their skills; in sports, in music, in art, the sciences, and overly involved with politics or other hobbies. Others are always on the internet, constantly watching TV, and like the world just enjoying life. Yes, a TC spends time on the above, but in moderation, and is busy doing God's Will.

10. A popular trend is to put tattoos on your body. A person with tattoos is not a sight to see, especially in their old age. Leviticus 19:28 says you shall not mark your body. The word 'shall' is used to express a command. Yes, some TC's have tattoos that were painted on before they were Born Again.

Leviticus 19:28 Do not cut your bodies for the dead or put tattoo marks on yourselves.

11. TC's aren't looking for popularity among their family or friends; their concentration is centered on pleasing God.

12. A TC hates evil.

Proverbs 8:13 - To fear the Lord is to hate evil; I hate pride and arrogance, evil behavior and perverse speech.

Psalms 97:10 - Let those who love the Lord hate evil, for he guards the lives of his faithful ones and delivers them from the hand of the wicked.

Romans 12:9 - Love must be sincere. Hate what is evil; cling to what is good.

13. TC's hate what is false.

Proverbs 13:5 - The righteous hate what is false, but the wicked make themselves a stench and bring shame upon themselves.

14. TC chooses his friends carefully.

Corinthians 15:33 - Do not be misled: "Bad company corrupts good character.

1 Corinthians 5:11 - ...I am writing to you that you must not associate with anyone who claims to be a brother or sister but is sexually immoral or greedy, an idolater or slanderer, a drunkard or swindler. Do not even eat with such people.

When you have God in your life and you put your full trust in Him, you begin to appreciate those around you and your surroundings.

15. A TC, with the help of the Holy Spirit, learns to be patient and to wait on God.

Philippians 4:6-7 - Do not be anxious about anything, but in every situation, by prayer and petition, with thanksgiving, present your requests to God. [7] And the peace of God, which transcends all understanding, will guard your hearts and your minds in Christ Jesus.

1 Peter 5:6 - **Humble yourselves; therefore, under God's mighty hand, that he may lift you up in due time.**

-Abraham waited 24 years for the son God promised him.

-Moses waited 40 years in the dessert, to get a glimpse of the Promise Land.

-Noah spent 100 years speaking to the people about the upcoming catastrophe, while building the ark.

-Joseph was sold by his brothers into slavery and was imprisoned for 13 years, before he was exalted in the Egyptian government.

16. A TC follows Jesus.

Mark 8:34-37 – Then, he called the crowd to him along with his disciples and said, "Whoever wants to be my disciple must deny themselves and take up their cross and follow me. For whoever wants to save their life will lose it, but whoever loses their life for me and for the gospel will save it. <u>What good is it for someone to gain the whole world, yet forfeit their soul? Or what can anyone give in exchange for their soul?</u>"

Do the Scriptures allow us to Judge?

1 Corinthians 6:2 - <u>Judging the world;</u> Or do you not know that the Lord's people will judge the world? And if you are to judge the world, are you not competent to judge trivial cases?

1 Corinthians 6:3 - <u>Judging angels</u>; Do you not know that we will judge angels? How much more the things of this life!

1 Corinthians 11:31 - <u>Judging yourself</u>; But if we were more discerning with regard to ourselves, we would not come under such judgment

John 7:24 - <u>Judge with righteousness</u>; Stop judging by mere appearances, but instead, judge correctly."

The following are judgmental calls you-yourself, are required to make:

2 Thessalonians 3:14 Take special note of anyone who does not obey our instruction in this letter. Do not associate with them, so that they may feel ashamed.

1 John 4:1 - Testing spirits-Dear friends, do not believe every spirit, but test the spirits to see whether they are from God, because many false prophets have gone out into the world.

Ephesians 5:11 - Have nothing to do with the fruitless deeds of darkness, but rather expose them.

1 Corinthians 15:33 - Do not be misled: "Bad company corrupts good character.

2 John 1:10 - If anyone comes to you and does not bring this teaching, do not take them into your house or welcome them.

1 Corinthians 5:11-12 - But now, I am writing to you that you must not associate with anyone who claims to be a brother or sister, but is sexually immoral or greedy, an idolater or slanderer, a drunkard or swindler. Do not even eat with such people.

Titus 3:9-11 - But avoid foolish controversies and genealogies and arguments and quarrels about the law, because these are unprofitable and useless. [10] Warn a divisive person once and then warn them a second time. After that, have nothing to do with them.

[11] You may be sure that such people are warped and sinful; they are self-condemned.

1 John 2:15-17 - Do not love the world or anything in the world. If anyone loves the world, love for the Father is not in them. [16] For everything in the world; the lust of the flesh, the lust of the eyes, and the pride of life—comes not from the Father but from the world. [17] The world and its desires pass away, but whoever does the will of God lives forever.

1 Tim 6:3-4 - If anyone teaches otherwise and does not agree to the sound instruction of our Lord Jesus Christ and to godly teaching, [4] they are conceited and understand nothing.

2 Thessalonians 3:6 - In the name of the Lord Jesus Christ, we command you, brothers and sisters, to keep away from every believer who is idle and disruptive and does not live according to the teaching you received from us.

2 Thessalonians 3:15 - Yet do not regard them as an enemy, but warn them as you would a fellow believer.

2 Corinthians 6:14 - Do not be yoked together with unbelievers. For what do righteousness and wickedness have in common? Or what fellowship can light have with darkness?

2 Corinthians 13:5 - Examine yourselves to see whether you are in the faith; test yourselves. Do you not realize that Christ Jesus is in you—unless, of course, you fail the test?

Acts 17:11 - Now the Berean Jews were of more noble character than those in Thessalonica, for they received the message with great eagerness and examined the Scriptures every day to see if what Paul said was true.

A person who is Born Again and has the Holy Spirit can say they are saved.

We are not allowed to judge others; people who we don't know if they're saved or not, whether they're alive or dead. This decision belongs to God alone. In our daily newspaper obituaries, some say that the people who died are now in Jesus' arms, others say they're singing with the angels. If the person who died did not announce he or she was saved, others shouldn't be making decisions that belong to God.

Romans 10:6-7 - But the righteousness that is by faith says: "Do not say in your heart, 'Who will ascend into heaven?'" (that is, to bring Christ down) [7] "or 'Who will descend into the deep?'" (that is, to bring Christ up from the dead).

How Pastors should present themselves

1. They should dress like Jesus and the Apostles did, who dressed the same as all the people they were preaching to. None of them had fancy vestments like robes, priestly outfits, and collars around their neck.

2. The Scriptures nowhere showed the Apostles, the Prophets, and Jesus having to entertain the people; with jokes, being a comedian, being loud and dancing around the stage, or saying things where they could fit in with the crowd. Jokes once in a while are fine, but what a pastor has to communicate as a representative of God is serious business.

3. Nowhere do we find in Scripture where Christian gatherings furnished promotions, like offering prizes, free drinks, and games if they came.

4. None of the Apostles, Prophets, or Jesus was financially wealthy.

Paul says in;

2 Corinthians 6:10 Sorrowful, yet always rejoicing; <u>poor, yet making many rich; having nothing, and yet possessing everything.</u>

1 Corinthians 9:14 - In the same way, the Lord has commanded that those who preach the gospel should receive their living from the gospel.

5. Pastors should be like the Apostle Paul and do whatever is necessary to save people, to bring them to Christ, and to follow the Bible.

Philippians 4:12 - I know what it is to be in need, and I know what it is to have plenty. I have learned the secret of being content in any and every situation, whether well fed or hungry, whether living in plenty or in want.

1 Corinthians 9:19-23 - Though I am free and belong to no one, I have made myself a slave to everyone, to win as many as possible. 20 To the Jews I became like a Jew, to win the Jews. To those under the law, I became like one under the law (though I myself am not under the law), so as to win those under the law. 21 To those not having the law I became like one not having the law (though I am not free from God's law but am under Christ's law), so as to win those not having the law. 22 To the weak I became weak, to win the weak. I have become all things to all people so that by all possible means I might save some. To the weak I became weak, to win the weak. I have become all things to all people so that by all possible means I might save some. 23 I do all this for the sake of the gospel that I may share in its blessings.

6. A good pastor should give talks on the pagan holidays!

7. Pastors should encourage their members to read the Bible every time they give a talk and tell their members to pray for discernment (spiritual guidance to understand the Bible, which leads to change).

8. And, instruct its members on How to defend the Truth.

9. Every time a pastor speaks, he should always talk about Repentance, Believing in the Truth, being Born Again, and receiving the Holy Spirit. This is the main goal in life for all people that want Everlasting Life with God.

Is Self-Defense and the Death Penalty Allowed in the Bible?

The main topics below come out of the pamphlet, "What Does the Bible Teach about Self-Defense? Can A Christian Use A Gun in Self Defense?" by David L. Brown. Ph.D.

The Second Amendment of the Constitution of the United States clearly states, "A well-regulated militia being necessary to the security of a Free State, the right of the People to keep and bear arms shall not be infringed."

What does the Bible say about?

Self-Defense

Luke 22:35-36 - **Speaking to the apostles**; then Jesus asked them, "When I sent you without purse, bag or sandals, did you lack anything?" [36] He said to them, "But now if you have a purse, take it, and also a bag; and if you don't have a sword, sell your cloak and buy one.

Matthew 26:52-54 - Put your sword back in its place, Jesus said to him, "for all who draw the sword will die by the sword. [53] Do you think I cannot call on my Father, and he will at once put at my disposal more than twelve legions of angels? [54] But how then would the Scriptures be fulfilled that say it must happen in this way?"

In the above Scripture, Jesus did not say they couldn't have weapons, only not to use them at the wrong time.

Exodus 22:2-3 - **Self-Defense**; if a thief is caught breaking in at night and is struck a fatal blow, the defender is not guilty of bloodshed; [3] but if it happens after sunrise, the defender is guilty of bloodshed. "Anyone who steals must certainly make restitution, but if they have nothing, they must be sold to pay for their theft.

The Death Penalty

Exodus 20:13 - You shall not murder.

Deuteronomy 5:17 - You shall not murder.

Exodus 21:12 **Anyone who strikes a person with a fatal blow is to be put to death.**

Deuteronomy 22:23-27 – **Rape**; if a man happens to meet in a town, a virgin pledged to be married, and he sleeps with her, [24] you shall take both of them to the gate of that town and stone them to death; the young woman because she was in a town and did not scream for help, and the man because he violated another man's wife. You must purge the evil from among you.

[25]But if out in the country, a man happens to meet a young woman pledged to be married and rapes her, only the man who has done this shall die. Do nothing to the woman; she has committed no sin deserving death. This case is like that of someone who attacks and murders a neighbor, [27] for the man found the young woman out in the country, and though the betrothed woman screamed, there was no one to rescue her.

Deuteronomy 27:25-27 - Cursed is anyone who accepts a bribe to kill an innocent person.

Leviticus 20:17 – **Incest**; If a man marries his sister, the daughter of either his father or his mother, and they have sexual relations, it is a disgrace. They are to be publicly removed from their people. He has dishonored his sister and will be held responsible.

Numbers 35:20-23 - **Accidental death**; if anyone with malice aforethought shoves another or throws something at them intentionally so that they die, [21] or if out of enmity one person hits another with their fist so that the other dies, that person is to be put to death; that person is a murderer. The avenger of blood shall put the murderer to death when they meet.

[22] But if without enmity someone suddenly pushes another or throws something at them unintentionally [23] or, without seeing them, drops on them a stone heavy enough to kill them, and they die, then since that other person was not an enemy and no harm was intended, the assembly must judge between the accused and the avenger of blood according to these regulations.

1 Samuel 25:13 - **Self-protection**; David said to his men, "Each of you, strap on your sword!"- So they did, and David strapped his on as well. About four hundred men went up with David, while two hundred stayed with the supplies.

In the Old Testament, one could receive the death penalty for over 30 crimes; which included murder, idolatry, the practice of magic, and blasphemy.

God is the first person in the whole world to come up with the death penalty and the right to carry arms. Who knows better than the Creator?

Assault weapons and large capacity magazines should be outlawed. And to make this new law effective and in conjunction with God's views, the criminals who are charged with killing someone- when using these weapons, should be charged with the death penalty with no appeals.

The government serves as God's agent for punishment of crimes, and includes the usage of the death penalty;

Romans 13:1-4 - Let everyone be subject to the governing authorities, for there is no authority except that which God has established. The authorities that exist have been established by God. ² Consequently, whoever rebels against the authority is rebelling against what God has instituted, and those who do so will bring judgment on themselves. ³ For rulers hold no terror for those who do right, but for those who do wrong. Do you want to be free from fear of the one in authority?

Then do what is right and you will be commended. For the one in authority is God's servant for your good. But if you do wrong, be afraid, for rulers do not bear the sword for no reason. They are God's servants, agents of wrath, to bring punishment on the wrongdoer.

Proverbs 6:16-25 - There are six things the Lord hates, seven that are detestable to him: ¹⁷ haughty eyes, a lying tongue, hands that shed innocent blood, ¹⁸ a heart that devises wicked schemes, feet that are quick to rush into evil, [19] a false witness who pours out lies and a person who stirs up conflict in the community.

Exodus 15:3 - The Lord is a warrior; the Lord is his name.

Does the New Testament allow the death penalty?

Matthew 15:4 - For God said, 'Honor your father and mother' and Anyone who curses their father or mother is to be put to death.

Matthew 7:2 - For in the same way you judge others, you will be judged, and with the measure you use, it will be measured to you.

Luke 11:21 - "When a strong man, fully armed, guards his own house, his possessions are safe.

Paul on the authority of the government

Romans 13:4 For the one in authority is God's servant for your good. But if you do wrong, be afraid, for rulers do not bear the sword for no reason. They are God's servants, agents of wrath to bring punishment on the wrongdoer.

Jesus and the Apostle Paul do not deny the right the government has on administering the death penalty. God gave the authority to governments to put to death people who commit murder, adultery, incest, rape, etc.

In fact, the United States was founded under the following Christian Biblical principles:

-We hold these truths to be self-evident, that all Men are created equal that are endowed by their creator with certain unalienable Rights that among these are Life, Liberty and the Pursuit of Happiness.

-We have "In God, we trust", on our money.

-In our pledge of allegiance "One nation under God".

Jesus says in Mark 12:17 "Give back to Cesar what is Cesar's and to God what is God's." That's why we pay taxes to fund the government.

Romans 13:1-2 - Let everyone be subject to the governing authorities, for there is no authority except that which God has established. The authorities that exist have been established by God. [2] Consequently, whoever rebels against the authority is rebelling against what God has instituted, and those who do so will bring judgment on themselves.

Romans 13:6 - This is also why you pay taxes, for the authorities are God's servants, who give their full time to governing.

Titus 3:1 - Remind the people to be subject to rulers and authorities, to be obedient, to be ready to do whatever is good.

- -

More on Governments

All around the world, one of the first things a tyrant leader (one who seizes power unconstitutionally or inherits the position) does, is to take away the guns from the people. This is a form of governmental control. We know that when citizens are not allowed to own weapons, the criminals are at a better advantage, because they're not going to give up their weapons.

God gave the Israelite leaders (the government) the power to raise an army and <u>recruit only men that are 21 years or older</u>. He also instructed the Israelites to send home for a year those who were just married, so they can make their wives happy and send home those with emotional problems. No wonder we have so many young men ages 17 to 20 who come home with emotional and psychological problems. God knew that at age 21 or more, men would be better equipped mentally. Just like when He told the Israelites to circumcise the babies at 8 days old, many specialists in this field today, will tell you that this is the day when the level of vitamin K is the highest, and that vitamin K plays a pivotal role in clotting, which helps to stop the bleeding.

Under the United States Constitution

The First Amendment states, "Congress shall not make any law respecting the establishment of religion." And "prohibiting the exercise there of".

The purpose of this law was to guarantee religious freedoms to all. Under the ruling parties of the old European countries, many of these nations/kingdoms followed only one Christian religion. The English were protestant and the French and Spanish were mainly catholic. <u>The new United States wanted a Christian country; however, they did not want their new country to have a dominant Christian religion</u>. Nowhere in the constitution will you see the term or concept "separation of church and state", it's a made-up word.

Education

The first public schools in America came about on April 23, 1635, in Boston, Massachusetts. The Puritans offered classes for boys only, from grades sixth through twelfth. The Puritans' main emphasis was to teach them to read, so the children could read the Bible.

The Public Schools in the United States have failed us in education; by teaching evolution (a theory that has been disapproved by many), critical race theory (promotes prejudices), and offering anti-Christian counseling services.

As my master's degree was in counseling, I know that these counseling theories promote the philosophy that you have the power to heal yourself of your troubles, rather than turning to God. God or Jesus is never mentioned in secular counseling. That's why I quit this degree at the tail-end of the requirements. The best place to take your children, if counseling is needed, is to your Bible Church or other biblical Christian resources.

Many will say that the best gift you can give your children is a good education. This is the second biggest myth or lie in the United States. The best gift you can give your children is a relationship with Jesus Christ. All other good things will follow.

We shouldn't follow when the governments, religions, or others, want us to do anything that is not in line with Scripture.

Refused to bow down and worship a pagan god;

For example, in Daniel chapter 3, Daniel's three friends refused to bow down and worship the king's [the government's] golden 90-foot high statue. The Babylonian government had them thrown in a burning furnace, but God rescued them.

Refused to stop teaching the Gospel;

Acts 4:5 - The next day, the rulers, the elders and the teachers [**the government and religion**] of the law met in Jerusalem.

Acts 4:16-21 – "What are we going to do with these men?" they asked. "Everyone living in Jerusalem knows they have performed a notable sign, and we cannot deny it. But to stop this thing from spreading any further among the people, we must warn them to speak no longer to anyone in this name." Then they called them in again and commanded them not to speak or teach at all in the name of Jesus. But Peter and John replied,

"Which is right in God's eyes? To listen to you, or to him? You be the judges! As for us, we cannot help speaking about what we have seen and heard."

After further threats, they let them go. They could not decide how to punish them, because all the people were praising God for what had happened.

Acts 4:25-27 - You spoke by the Holy Spirit through the mouth of your servant, our father David: "Why do the nations rage and the people plot in vain? [26] The kings of the earth rise up and the rulers band together against the Lord and against his anointed one? [27] Indeed Herod and Pontius Pilate [the government] met together with the Gentiles and the people of Israel in this city to conspire against your holy servant Jesus, whom you anointed.

Revelations 13:11-17 - Then I saw a second beast, coming out of the earth. It had two horns like a lamb, but it spoke like a dragon. It exercised all the authority of the first beast on its behalf <u>and made the earth and its inhabitants worship the first beast</u> [**a new worldwide government**], whose fatal wound had been healed. And it performed great signs, even causing fire to come down from heaven to the earth in full view of the people. Because of the signs, it was given the power to perform on behalf of the first beast, it deceived the inhabitants of the earth. It ordered them to set up an image in honor of the beast who was wounded by the sword and yet lived.

The second beast was given the power to give breath to the image of the first beast so that the image could speak and cause all who refused to worship the image to be killed. <u>It also forced all people, great and small, rich and poor, free and slave, to receive a mark on their right hands or on their foreheads [from the government]</u>, so that they could not buy or sell unless they had the mark, which is the name of the beast or the number of its name.

As True Christians, we should not support anything that goes against the Truth (Bible), which includes Abortion, Transgenderism, Homosexuality, Same-Sex Marriage and the Right to Die. The right to die issue goes against the Bible because God has preset a day for us to die. Also, when a person is suffering, many will turn to God and can be saved.

The Christian community has also seen a Colorado Baker who refused to make the wedding cake for a gay wedding and pastors all around the United States, who have refused to marry gay couples. Here in New Mexico, Elane Photography refused to photograph a gay marriage.

The Democratic politicians;

The Democratic platform in 2016 said, "We believe unequivocally" … including safe and legal abortion…Democrats believe that LGBT rights are human rights…

The problem with these people is that they think they know more about what's good for a person than God, who created all things. They follow a mentality that says, "What is said to be good is bad and what is said to be bad is good." They work against God.

As years passed, the United States government and many of its citizens have been supporting these non-biblical concepts, thus deteriorating the blessings from God.

The United States government has promoted a welfare state; free food stamps, free medical services for many, free public housing, or at a reduced rate.

Scripture requires Christians and the Church; to feed the hungry, clothe the naked, help the sick, visit those in prison and take care of widows. The government's job according to Scripture is to protect its citizenry and punish the criminals. Of course, there are many Churches and organizations that fulfill their responsibilities, yet there are many others, especially individual Christians, that sit back and let the government handle these needs.

James 1:27 – **Orphans and widows**; religion that God our Father accepts as pure and faultless is this: to look after orphans and widows in their distress and to keep oneself from being polluted by the world.

Leviticus 19:9-10 - **Sharing with others**; when you reap the harvest of your land, do not reap to the very edges of your field or gather the gleanings of your harvest. [10] Do not go over your vineyard a second time or pick up the grapes that have fallen. Leave them for the poor and the foreigner. I am the Lord your God.

Deuteronomy 15:7 **Be good to the poor**- if anyone is poor among your fellow Israelites in any of the towns of the land the Lord your God is giving you, do not be hardhearted or tightfisted toward them.

Proverbs 31:8-9 - **Defend the right of the poor and needy**-; speak up for those who cannot speak for themselves, for the rights of all who are destitute. Speak up and judge fairly; defend the rights of the poor and needy.

1 Timothy 6:17-18 - **Command those who are rich;** in this present world, not to be arrogant nor to put their hope in wealth, which is so uncertain, but to put their hope in God, who richly provides us with everything for our enjoyment. [18] **Command them to do good, to be**

rich in good deeds, and to be generous and willing to share. [19] In this way they will lay up treasure for themselves as a firm foundation for the coming age, so that they may take hold of the life that is truly life.

Matthew 25:35-40 - For I was hungry and you gave me something to eat, I was thirsty and you gave me something to drink, I was a stranger and you invited me in, [36] I needed clothes and you clothed me, I was sick and you looked after me, I was in prison and you came to visit me.

[37] Then the righteous will answer him, 'Lord, when did we see you hungry and feed you, or thirsty and give you something to drink? When did we see you a stranger and invite you in, or needing clothes and clothe you? [39] When did we see you sick or in prison and go to visit you? [40] The King will reply, "Truly I tell you, whatever you did for one of the least of these brothers and sisters of mine, you did for me."

The Governments of the world have spent trillions of dollars in trying to control problems of poverty, troubled youth, homelessness, crime, mental health, drug problems, etc. with very little success. The government's biggest problem is that their programs are anti-Christian; Doubt, Addictions, Depression, Anxiety, Homosexuality, Abortion, Mental problems, Anger problems, and Dumbness, are all Spiritual problems and should be dealt with as such, through God, with support from Christian people and Christian organizations.

By Dumbness, I mean they don't really feel and appreciate the people and the beauty of God's creations around them. They have a feeling of a rush to finish their chores, to see the day go by fast each day at the job, and earn as much money as possible. The result is; the years pass by fast, and before they know it (those that are still alive), there old and gray, saying, "Where did the time go?"

Currently, the government wants everyone to get the Corona virus shot. When these vaccines were in the early stages of testing or development, manufacturers used human baby tissues or cells from an abortion. Some Christians are against this shot for that reason, others because of the unknown future side effects, etc.

A good reason against the shot is found in;

Psalm 91:1-7 - Whoever dwells in the shelter of the Most High will rest in the shadow of the Almighty.

[2] I will say of the Lord, "He is my refuge and my fortress, my God, in whom I trust."

[3] **Surely he will save you from the fowler's snare and from the deadly pestilence.** [4] He will cover you with his feathers, and under his wings, you will find refuge; his faithfulness will be your shield and rampart.

You will not fear the terror of night, nor the arrow that flies by day [6] nor the pestilence that stalks in the darkness, nor the plague that destroys at midday.

[7] **A thousand may fall at your side, ten thousand at your right hand, but it will not come near you.**

Put your trust in God and He will protect you.

Are Tithing's (Contributions) Mandatory?

Yes, in the Old Testament, it was a command. The tithings provided for the Levitical Priesthood, festivals, and the poor. The tithings to God were not a gift it was a command.

Leviticus 27:30-34 - A tithe of everything from the land, whether grain from the soil or fruit from the trees, belongs to the Lord; it is holy to the Lord. [31] Whoever would redeem any of their tithes must add a fifth of the value to it. [32] Every tithe of the herd and flock—every tenth animal that passes under the shepherd's rod—will be holy to the Lord.

[33] No one may pick out the good from the bad or make any substitution. If anyone does make a substitution, both the animal and its substitute become holy and cannot be redeemed.' [34] These are the commands the Lord gave Moses at Mount Sinai for the Israelites.

The first ten percent was considered holy and belonged to God. Israelites could give ten percent in crops, livestock, etc. Also, they could give money instead, which would increase the payment to twelve percent.

When it came to livestock, a shepherd had to set aside every tenth for God. It was decided by simply counting the animals and consecrating every tenth.

Numbers 18:26 - Speak to the Levites and say to them: When you receive from the Israelites the tithe I give you as your inheritance, you must present a tenth of that tithe as the Lord's offering.

From the income that the Levites received from the tithe, they were still responsible for giving 10 percent off the top to God.

Israelites also tithed to support a special jubilee festival (Deuteronomy chapter 1), and took a third tithe every three years to take care of orphans, widows, and the poor (Deuteronomy chapter 14). These mandatory offerings averaged out to about 23 percent of their income a year.

Deuteronomy 14:22 - Be sure to set aside a tenth of all that your fields produce each year.

Deuteronomy 14:28-29 - At the end of every three years, bring all the tithes of that year's produce and store it in your towns, [29] so that the Levites (who have no allotment or inheritance of their own) and the foreigners, the fatherless and the widows who live in your towns may come and eat and be satisfied, and so that the Lord your God may bless you in all the work of your hands.

Tithings in the New Testament are not a command

Matthew 6:1-4 - Be careful not to practice your righteousness in front of others to be seen by them. If you do, you will have no reward from your Father in heaven.

[2] "So when you give to the needy, do not announce it with trumpets, as the hypocrites do in the synagogues and on the streets, to be honored by

others. Truly I tell you, they have received their reward in full. [3] But when you give to the needy, do not let your left hand know what your right hand is doing, [4] so that your giving may be in secret. Then your Father, who sees what is done in secret, will reward you."

Matthew 6:19-21 - Do not store up for yourselves treasures on earth, where moths and vermin destroy, and where thieves break in and steal. [20] But store up for yourselves treasures in heaven, where moths and vermin do not destroy, and where thieves do not break in and steal. [21] For where your treasure is, there your heart will be also.

1 Timothy 6:17-19 - Command those who are rich in this present world not to be arrogant nor to put their hope in wealth, which is so uncertain, but to put their hope in God, who richly provides us with everything for our enjoyment. [18] Command them to do good, to be rich in good deeds, and to be generous and willing to share. [19] In this way they will lay up treasure for themselves as a firm foundation for the coming age, so that they may take hold of the life that is truly life.

2 Corinthians 8:12 - **The gift is acceptable according to what one has, not according to what he does not have.**

2 Corinthians 9:7 – **Each man should give what he has decided in his heart to give, not reluctantly, or under compulsion, for God loves a cheerful giver.**

Malachi 3:10 - Bring the whole tithe into the storehouse, that there may be food in my house. Test me in this," says the Lord Almighty, "and see if I will not throw open the floodgates of heaven and pour out so much blessing that there will not be room enough to store it.

Those that tithe, according to Malachi, receive a blessing from the Almighty God.

Tithing, witnessing the Truth to others, and helping others in need for the glory of God, are good ways to please God.

With tithing, don't let your left hand know what your right hand is doing - Matthew 6:3. Give in secret so God can reward you - Matthew 6:4.

Give your tithing's to the church, organization, or worthy cause, that follows Scripture, and that feeds you the Truth.

Why did God create us?

For His glory

Isaiah 43:7 - Everyone who is called by my name, whom I created for my glory, whom I formed and made.

He made us to be a chosen race, a royal priesthood

1 Peter 2:9 - But you are a chosen people, a royal priesthood, a holy nation, God's special possession, that you may declare the praises of him who called you out of darkness into his wonderful light.

He formed us for Himself

Isaiah 43:21 – The people I formed for myself that they may proclaim my praise.

We are His

Psalms 100:3 - Know that the Lord is God. It is he who made us, and we are his; we are his people, the sheep of his pasture.

He cared for us before we were even born

Isaiah 44:2 - This is what the Lord says—he who made you, who formed you in the womb, and who will help you do not be afraid, Jacob, my servant, Jeshurun, whom I have chosen.

He cared for us and loved us

Isaiah 46:3 - Listen to me, you descendants of Jacob, all the remnant of the people of Israel, you whom I have upheld since your birth, and have carried since you were born.

We are considered important of all things He made

James 1:18 - He chose to give us birth through the word of truth, that we might be a kind of first fruits of all he created.

He loved us so much; He made us in His own image

Genesis 1:27 - So God created mankind in his own image, in the image of God he created them; male and female he created them.

We are His workmanship

Ephesians 2:10 - For we are God's handiwork, created in Christ Jesus to do good works, which God prepared in advance for us to do.

And because of Man's fall, He wants to redeem us from all wickedness

Titus 2:14 - who gave himself for us to redeem us from all wickedness and to purify for himself a people that are his very own, eager to do what is good.

He has made big plans for us

Jeremiah 29:11 - "For I know the plans I have for you", declares the Lord, plans to prosper you and not to harm you, plans to give you hope and a future.

Everything He created is Good

1 Timothy 4:4 - For everything God created is good, and nothing is to be rejected if it is received with thanksgiving.

How to Live and Relate to Others

- Philippians 2:3 - Do nothing out of selfish ambition or vain conceit. Rather, in humility, value others above yourself.

- James 4:10 - Humble yourself before the Lord, and he will lift you up.

- Psalms 37:7-8 – Do not fret when men succeed in their ways. Do not fret it only leads to evil.

- Philippians 3:13 – Stay away from argument and complaining.

- 1 Thessalonians 4:11 - Mind your own business.

- 1 Tim 5:8 - Worse than unbelievers are those who do not provide for his relatives, especially for his immediate family.

- 2 Corinthians 6:14 - Stay away from unbelievers, <u>unless you're witnessing to them.</u>

- Hebrews 12:14 - Make every effort to live in peace with all men.

- Hebrews 13:6 – Do not forget to do good and share with others.

- 2 Timothy 2:23 - Have nothing to do with foolish and stupid arguments, because you know they produce quarrels.

- 1 Peter 2:17 – Show proper respect to everyone.

- Romans 12:18 - Live at peace with everyone.

- Romans 12:17-21 - Repay no one evil for evil, but give thought to do what is honorable in the sight of all. If possible, so far as it depends on you, live peaceably with all. Beloved, never avenge yourselves, but leave it to the wrath of God, for it is written, "Vengeance is mine, I will repay, says the Lord."

- Matthew 5:38-39 - "You have heard that it was said, 'An eye for an eye and a tooth for a tooth.' But I say to you, do not resist the one who is evil. But if anyone slaps you on the right cheek, turn to him the other also.

- Isaiah 43:18 – Forget the former things. Do not dwell on the past.

- Proverbs 12:13 - Whoever loves discipline loves knowledge, but whoever hates correction is stupid.

- Proverbs 13:10 - Where there is strife, there is pride, but wisdom is found in those who take advice.

- Mathew 6:3-4 do not let your left hand know what your right hand is doing so that your giving will be in secret

- Deuteronomy 23:19 - You shall not charge interest on loans to your brother.

- Leviticus 25:26 - take no interest from him, or profit, but fear your God, that your brother may live beside you.

- Luke 6:34-35 – If you lend to those from whom you expect to receive, what credit is that to you? Even sinners lend to sinners, to get back the same amount. But love your enemies, and do good, and lend expecting nothing in return, and your reward will be great, and you will be sons of the Most High, for he is kind to the ungrateful and the evil.

- Proverbs 20:19 - Avoid a man who talks too much.

- Proverbs 22:24 - Do not make friends with a hot-tempered man. Do not associate with one easily angered or you may learn his ways and get yourself ensnared.

- Matthew 7:12 - Do to others what you would want them to do to you. This sums up the laws of the prophets.

- Proverbs 28:26 - He who trusts in himself is a fool.

Giving in Secret

Matthew 6:1 - Jesus says, Beware of practicing your righteousness before men to be noticed by them; otherwise, you have no reward with your Father who is in heaven.

Matthew 6:2 - So when you give to the poor, do not sound a trumpet before you, as the hypocrites do in the synagogues and in the streets, so that they may be honored by men. Truly I say to you, they have their reward in full.

Matthew 6:3–4 - He says, "when you give to the poor, do not let your left hand know what your right hand is doing so that your giving will be in secret; your Father, who sees what is done in secret will reward you."

Put value into your Life

Luke 6:32 - If you love those who love you- what is that to you? Even the sinners love those who love them. If you do good to those who are good to you, what credit is that to you? Even the sinners do that.

Do we need to Congregate with other Christians?

Some say it's not necessary to go to church. Others say, praying and reading Christian writings is sufficient.

What does the Bible say?

Acts 9:31 - Then the church throughout Judea, Galilee, and Samaria enjoyed a time of peace and was strengthened. Living in the fear of the Lord and encouraged by the Holy Spirit, it increased in numbers.

Acts 11:25-26 - Then, Barnabas went to Tarsus to look for Saul, [26] and when he found him, he brought him to Antioch. So for a whole year, Barnabas and Saul met with the church and taught great numbers of people. The disciples were called Christians first at Antioch.

Romans 12:4-5 For just as each of us has one body with many members, and these members do not all have the same function, [5] so in Christ, we, though many, form one body, and each member belongs to all the others.

Hebrews 10:24-25 - And let us consider how we may spur one another on toward love and good deeds, [25] not giving up meeting together, as some are in the habit of doing, but encouraging one another and all the more, as you see the Day approaching.

Ephesians 4:14-16 - Then we will no longer be infants, tossed back and forth by the waves, and blown here and there by every wind of teaching and by the cunning and craftiness of people in their deceitful scheming. [15] Instead, speaking the truth in love, we will grow to become in every respect the mature body of him who is the head, that is, Christ. [16] <u>From him the whole body, joined and held together by every supporting ligament, grows and builds itself up in love, as each part does its work</u>.

How can Believers be in the World and not of the World?

1 John 2:15-17 - Do not love the world or anything in the world. <u>If anyone loves the world, love for the Father is not in them</u>. [16] <u>For everything in the world; the lust of the flesh, the lust of the eyes, and the pride of life—comes not from the Father but from the world</u>. [17] The world and its desires pass away, but whoever does the will of God lives forever.

Colossians 3:2-5 - <u>Set your minds on things above</u>, not on earthly things. [3] For you died, and your life is now hidden with Christ in God. [4] When Christ, who is your life, appears, then you also will appear with him in glory.

[5] <u>Put to death, therefore, whatever belongs to your earthly nature</u>: sexual immorality, impurity, lust, evil desires, and greed, which is idolatry.

Matthew 6:19 - Do not store up for yourselves treasures on earth, where moths and vermin destroy, and where thieves break in and steal.

Matthew 6:24 - No one can serve two masters. Either you will hate the one and love the other, or you will be devoted to the one and despise the other. <u>You cannot serve both God and money.</u>

Matthew 16:26 - Look at the birds of the air; they do not sow or reap or store away in barns, and yet your heavenly Father feeds them. Are you not much more valuable than they?

2 Corinthians 4:18 - So we fix our eyes not on what is seen, but on what is unseen since what is seen is temporary, but what is unseen is eternal.

John 15:18-19 - <u>If the world hates you, keep in mind that it hated me first</u>. [19] If you belonged to the world, it would love you as its own. As it is, you do not belong to the world, but I have chosen you out of the world. That is why the world hates you.

Health Benefits

Nowadays we have to be careful with what foods we eat. Many of the products are grown with the usage of laboratory additives (rather than letting them grow as God intended), and have pesticides. When these foods are harvested, they add many laboratory ingredients, additives, and colors, to help preserve them, to make them more attractive and so they'll taste better. There are many scientists who will say that these additives are causing all kinds of neurological and physical problems.

The government knows this and has taken certain additives off the market, but certainly not all of them. The government does not take them all off, because they know that they wouldn't be able to feed the masses. Buy organic at Market Street, and Trader Joe's. They have hundreds and hundreds of organic products, and they aren't as expensive as the other organic stores.

Good advice from God concerning your health;

Genesis 9:2-3 - The fear and dread of you will fall on all the beasts of the earth, and on all the birds in the sky, on every creature that moves along the ground, and on all the fish in the sea; they are given into your hands. [3] Everything that lives and moves about will be food for you. <u>Just as I gave you the green plants, I now give you everything.</u>

Proverbs 24:13 - <u>Eat honey</u>, my son, for it is good; honey from the comb is sweet to your taste.

Proverbs 25:27 - <u>It is not good to eat too much honey</u>…

Matthew 4:4 - Jesus answered, It is written: <u>Man shall not live on bread alone, but on every word that comes from the mouth of God.</u>

Romans 14:20 - Do not destroy the work of God for the sake of food. All food is clean, but it is wrong for a person to eat anything that causes someone else to stumble.

1 Corinthians 10:31 - So whether you eat or drink or whatever you do, do it all for the glory of God.

1 Corinthians 6:12-13 - I have the right to do anything, you say, but not everything is beneficial. "I have the right to do anything"—but I will not be mastered by anything. [13] You say, "Food for the stomach and the stomach for food, and God will destroy them both." The body, however, is not meant for sexual immorality but for the Lord, and the Lord for the body.

1 Corinthians 6:19 - Do you not know that your bodies are temples of the Holy Spirit, who is in you, whom you have received from God? You are not your own.

1 Timothy 4:1-5 - The Spirit clearly says that in later times some will abandon the faith and follow deceiving spirits and things taught by demons. [2] Such teachings come through hypocritical liars, whose consciences have been seared as with a hot iron. [3] They forbid people to marry and order them to abstain from certain foods, which God created to be received with thanksgiving by those who believe and who know the truth.

[4] For everything God created is good, and nothing is to be rejected if it is received with thanksgiving, [5] because it is consecrated by the word of God and prayer.

1 Timothy 5:23 – Stop drinking only water, and use a little wine because of your stomach and your frequent illnesses.

Why is it so Important to forgive others?

If we forgive people of their sins, the act of forgiveness opens up doors where the person who sinned, has an opportunity to praise God because of your beliefs, and allows them to follow and grow in God's love. God forgave us of our sins by giving us his Son as the perfect unblemished sacrifice. If you say the "Our Father Prayer" and you don't forgive another for his or her sins, God won't forgive you. Forgiveness is one the most important undertakings a human can do because forgiveness helps you in your spiritual growth, and to be a man and woman in God's eyes.

Matthew 6:9-13 - This, then, is how you should pray:

Our Father in heaven,

hallowed be your name,

[10] your kingdom come,

your will be done,

on earth as it is in heaven.

[11] Give us today our daily bread.

[12] And forgive us our debts,

as we also have forgiven our debtors.

[13] And lead us not into temptation,

but deliver us from the evil one

Matthew 6:14 - For if you forgive other people when they sin against you, your heavenly Father will also forgive you.

Matthew 18:22 - Jesus answered, "I tell you, not seven times, but seventy-seven times (meaning you forgive them always)."

Matthew 18:32-35 – Then, the master called the servant in. You wicked servant, he said, "I canceled all that debt of yours because you begged me to. [33] Shouldn't you have had mercy on your fellow servant just as I had on you?" [34] In anger his master handed him over to the jailers to be tortured, until he should pay back all he owed.

³⁵ This is how my heavenly Father will treat each of you unless you forgive your brother or sister from your heart.

1 Peter 4:8 - Above all, love each other deeply, because love covers over a multitude of sins.

Six good reasons to forgive;

The Prodigal Son in Luke 15:11-32;

The younger son asked his father for his inheritance and squandered it on good times. When the money ran out and a severe famine hit, he was hungry. He took on a job, feeding pigs and eating what the pigs ate, which is a detestable thing for an Israelite to do.

When he came to his senses, he told his father he was no longer worthy to be a son and that he had sinned against his father and heaven, and asked his father to give him a job like the other hired hands.

<u>His father forgave him</u>, even though the financial loss was great. The father said, 'My son was dead and now is alive, he was lost and now is found, let's celebrate.'

The other older son was not invited to the celebration, and was not happy to see how his father handled the situation, or to see his lost brother. What many don't know is that this son was also lost. Over the years, he did what his father told him to do, for his own benefit. Both sons were lost, and only one was found.

Joseph, the son of Jacob and Rachel, sold into slavery;

In the story of Joseph, who told his brothers and father about his two dreams out of excitement, yet they did not like his dreams.

Genesis 37:5-11 - Joseph had a dream, and when he told it to his brothers, they hated him all the more. ⁶ He said to them, "Listen to this dream I had: ⁷ We were binding sheaves of grain out in the field when, suddenly, my sheaf rose and stood upright, while your sheaves gathered around mine and bowed down to it. ⁸ His brothers said to him, "Do you intend to reign over us? Will you actually rule us?" And they hated him all the more because of his dream and what he had said. Then he had another dream, and he told it to his brothers. "Listen," he said, "I had another dream, and this time, the sun and moon and eleven stars were bowing down to me. ¹⁰ When he told his father as well as his brothers, his father rebuked him and said, "What is this dream you had? Will your mother and I and your brothers actually come and bow down to the ground before you?" ¹¹ His brothers were jealous of him, but his father kept the matter in mind.

Joseph's brothers were jealous of Joseph not only because of this dream, but because the father favored him. Any child growing up in a household that is favored over the other siblings causes a lot of emotional problems. So, Joseph was sold into slavery by his brothers. While being a slave in Egypt, Joseph was falsely accused of attempted rape and thrown into prison.

Joseph, while in prison, was called by the Pharaoh to interpret his dreams.

Genesis 41:15-16 - Pharaoh said to Joseph, "I had a dream, and no one can interpret it. But I have heard it said of you that when you hear a dream you can interpret it." ¹⁶ "I cannot do it," Joseph replied to Pharaoh, "but God will give Pharaoh the answer he desires."

After this interpretation, Joseph was elevated to second in command of Egypt, because he saved Egypt from a disastrous famine.

Genesis 45:5 - [Joseph speaking to his brothers] "And now, do not be distressed and do not be angry with yourselves for selling me here, because it was to save lives that God sent me ahead of you."

After all that Joseph went through; slavery, being accused of attempted rape, and being imprisoned, he forgave his brothers and kept his faith and trust in God.

Stephen;

Stephen, who was among seven chosen to help distribute food to the widows;

Acts 6:3-15 – "Brothers and sisters, choose seven men from among you who are known to be full of the Spirit and wisdom. We will turn this responsibility over to them [4] and will give our attention to prayer and the ministry of the word." [5] This proposal pleased the whole group. They chose Stephen, a man full of faith and the Holy Spirit; also Philip, Procorus, Nicanor, Timon, Parmenas, and Nicolas from Antioch, a convert to Judaism. [6] They presented these men to the apostles, who prayed and laid their hands on them. Now Stephen, a man full of God's grace and power, performed great wonders and signs among the people.

[9] Opposition arose, however, from members of the Synagogue of the Freedmen (as it was called)—Jews of Cyrene and Alexandria as well as the provinces of Cilicia and Asia—who began to argue with Stephen. [10] But they could not stand up against the wisdom the Spirit gave him as he spoke. [11] Then they secretly persuaded some men to say, "We have heard Stephen speak blasphemous words against Moses and against God." [12] So, they stirred up the people and the elders and the teachers of the law. They seized Stephen and brought him before the Sanhedrin. They produced false witnesses, who testified, "This fellow never stops speaking against this holy place and the law. [14] For we have heard him say that this Jesus of Nazareth will destroy this place and change the customs Moses handed down to us." Stephen was stoned to death just for speaking the Truth about Jesus.

Acts 7:59 - While they were stoning him, Stephen prayed, "Lord Jesus, receive my spirit." Then he fell on his knees and cried out, "<u>Lord, do not hold this sin against them</u>." When he had said this, he fell asleep.

Jesus' life on earth;

Luke 7:44-47 - Then he turned toward the woman and said to Simon, "Do you see this woman? I came into your house. You did not give me any water for my feet, but she wet my feet with her tears and wiped them with her hair. [45] You did not give me a kiss, but this woman, from the time I entered, has not stopped kissing my feet. [46] You did not put oil on my head, but she has poured perfume on my feet. [47] <u>Therefore, I tell you, her many sins have been forgiven</u>, as her great love has shown. But whoever has been forgiven little loves little."

Luke 23:34 - Jesus said, "<u>Father, forgive them, for they do not know what they are doing</u>." And they divided up his clothes by casting lots.

The sins of all the many people Jesus healed while on earth, were forgiven, otherwise, they wouldn't have been healed.

The father who forgave a boy for killing his boy;

There was a single man, about 20 years ago, who had a pre-teen son and daughter. Down the street, a grandma and grandpa took in one of their pre-teen grandsons, because he was always in trouble and the parents couldn't handle him. When school started, the boy began to cause trouble among the students. The boy who lived close to him, stayed as far from him as possible.

One day the school had a homecoming celebration, with a bonfire. The bully confronted his neighbor and argued with him. Then, the bully hit him over the head with a thick branch and killed him. The bully, now a murderer, was charged and sentenced to a juvenile correction facility. The single father lost his only son.

Several months later, the father decided to send the murderer a letter. The murderer responded to his letter. Then they started to send letters to each other. Six months later, the father started to visit the murderer regularly. After a year, the dead boy's father asked the killer's parents if he could adopt their son. They gladly transferred custody and he adopted the murderer.

The father took a big risk because he had a pre-teen daughter at home. When the boy was released from the juvenile correction facility, he went to live with his new father and sister. He was no longer a murderer; he was a son. Years later, one of the neighbors asked the father, which son he loved the most? The father said, "I love them both the same. They're both my sons!"

A Christian Pastor in Korea;

During the Korean War, a pastor in a small rural village awoke one morning to find that his young son, his only child, had been killed. Apparently, some soldiers had slipped in during the night and randomly executed a number of villagers in a brutal act of terrorism.

The pastor was beside himself with grief. He had looked forward to his son someday following in his footsteps and becoming a pastor. Now, his friends feared for his emotional stability, so severe was the grief he experienced over the boy's senseless death. It seemed so cruel, so unjust. His son was not in the army; he posed no threat to anyone. Why should he have been singled out like this?

Finally, the Korean pastor decided what he must do in return for this act of violence. He announced that he would hunt down the men who had killed his son and would not give up until he had found them. No obstacle would stand in his way, no hardship would deter him. This grief-stricken father resolved to do whatever it took.

Amazingly, he was able to learn the identities of the two terrorists, slip behind enemy lines, and found out where they lived. Early one morning, he snuck into their house and confronted them. The pastor told them who he was and that he knew they had murdered his son. "You owe me a debt," he said to them. "I have come to collect it."

The two young men were obviously expecting to be killed in retaliation. But the pastor's next words astonished them. "You have taken my son," he said, "and now I want you to become my sons in his place."

The pastor stayed with them for several days, until he was able to persuade them to come with him. In time he adopted them as his legal sons. He loved them and cared for them. They became Christians, went to seminary, and were ordained. Today, those two men are pastors in Korea, all because of a father who was willing to do whatever it took to win them, whose love was utterly unstoppable.

How to defend the Truth (the Word of God in the Bible)

From the book "Fast Facts on False Teachings" by Ron Carlson and Ed Decker, with the exception of comments at the end.

Paul says in 2 Timothy 2:15, "Do your best to present yourself to God as one approved, a workman who does not need to be ashamed and who correctly handles the Word of truth," and in 4:2 he says, "Preach the Word, be prepared in season and out of season, correct, rebuke and encourage, with great patience and careful instruction."

Peter says in 1 Peter 3:15, "In your heart set apart Christ as Lord. Always be prepared to give an answer to everyone who asks you to give the reason for the hope that you have."

What Jesus called the religious leaders of his days, in Matthew 12:34: "You brood of vipers, how can you who are evil say anything good? For the mouth speaks what the heart is full of." And what Jesus said to the Pharisees in Mathew 15:7: "You hypocrites! Isaiah was right when he prophesied about you."

1. Don't be ashamed to speak about the gospel - Romans 1:16.

2. There is only one true God - Deuteronomy 6:4, Isaiah 43:10-11, and 1 Corinthians 8:4.

3. God is a Spirit who fills the heavens - Jeremiah 23:24 and John 4:24.

4. God is not a human living man - Numbers 23:19, Job 9:32, and Hosea 11:9.

5. Jesus is the Almighty God manifested in the flesh - John 1:1-3, 14 and 18, Colossians 1:15-17, and 1 Timothy 3:16.

6. Jesus preexisted in heaven, man didn't - John 8:23, 1 Corinthians 15:46-49, Genesis 2:7, and Zechariah 12:1, 10.

7. We became, children of God by adoption - Romans 8:14-16, Galatians 4:5-6, and Ephesians 1:5.

8. The gospel(good news), by which we are saved, is that Jesus provided forgiveness of sins and eternal life through his finished work - 1 Corinthians 15:1-4, Hebrews 1:3, John 19:30, and Colossians 1:20-22.

9. We are saved by grace through faith unto good works as God's workmanship - Ephesians 2:8-10.

10. God makes us good creatures as the author and finisher of our faith - 2 Corinthians 5:17-21 and Hebrews 12:2.

What are the dangers of being a Lukewarm Christian in the Bible?

Revelation 3:15-16 - I know your deeds, that you are neither cold nor hot. I wish you were either one or the other! [16] So, because you are lukewarm, neither hot nor cold, **I am about to spit you out of my mouth.**

1 John 2:15-16 - Do not love the world or anything in the world. If anyone loves the world, love for the Father is not in them. [16] For everything in the world; the lust of the flesh, **the lust of the eyes, and the pride of life, comes not from the Father but from the world.**

Titus 1:16 - **They claim to know God, but by their actions they deny him**. They are detestable, disobedient, and unfit for doing anything good.

Matthew 7:21-23 - Not everyone who says to me, 'Lord, Lord,' will enter the kingdom of heaven, but only the one who does the will of my Father who is in heaven.

[22] **Many will say to me on that day, Lord, Lord, did we not prophesy in your name and in your name drive out demons and in your name**

perform many miracles?' ²³ Then I will tell them plainly, I never knew you. Away from me, you evildoers!

Luke 6:46 - Why do you call me, 'Lord, Lord,' **and do not do what I say?**

1 Corinthians 13:2 - If I have the gift of prophecy and can fathom all mysteries and all knowledge, and if I have a faith that can move mountains, but do not have love, I am nothing.

2 Corinthians 13:5 - Examine yourselves to see whether you are in the faith; test yourselves. **Do you not realize that Christ Jesus is in you, unless, of course, you fail the test?**

Isaiah 29:13 - These people come near to me with their mouth and honor me with their lips, but their hearts are far from me. **Their worship of me is based on merely human rules they have been taught.**

— —

Many Republican politicians in the United States are lukewarm. Yes, they don't support Homosexuality, Abortion, Transgenderism, and the Right to Die. However, they don't speak up for the Truth in their positions as representatives. I guess they think they're not allowed to, since many Americans believe in a concept called "Separation of Church and State", which isn't found in the constitution. The constitution is their Bible, for quite a few of these Republicans and many of the Democratic politicians. Democrats are nowhere close to being Lukewarm.

Many Christian businesses claim to be Christians, but if you visit their stores, there are no outwardly signs. At the least, they could have a stand inside their stores, offering a leaflet on <u>who Jesus is and how to be saved and inherit everlasting life</u>.

CHAPTER 9

VARIOUS SINFUL TOPICS

Sections that are highlighted come from the book "Quick Answers to Social Issues", by Bryan Osborne.

What does the Bible say about Homosexuality, Transgenderism, Racism, Abortion, and Slavery?

Homosexuality

Genesis 19:4 - <u>All the men from every part of the city of Sodom - both young and old </u>- surrounded the house, where the two angels (disguised as men) were staying. The men called out "Where are the men who came to you tonight?" Genesis 19:5 - "…Bring them out to us, so that we can have sex with them."

Sodomy is when two men have anal sex. The men, young and old, of all parts of the town wanted to gang rape the angels. In Genesis 19:11, the angels blinded the men, young and old, before the mob could take other measures like breaking down the door.

God, being all-knowing (omniscient), knew the sins of Sodom and Gomorrah. Many Scriptures show the displeasure and anger God has against homosexuality.

So, this would have been their primary sin against God. Notice again, in the story above, where all the old and young men of the town wanted to have sex with them. This evil desire to have ungodly sex was so great; the angels had to blind them. This story tells us that homosexuality can lead to overwhelming emotions for the need for sex at any cost.

In Leviticus 20:13, God calls this act of homosexuality detestable.

Judges 19:16-25 -I In the town of Gibeah, while they were enjoying themselves, some of the wicked men of the city surrounded the house. Pounding on the door, they shouted to the old man who owned the house. "Bring out the man who came to your house so we can have sex with him." The owner of the house pleaded with the wicked men, to no avail, and offered his virgin daughter and his concubine. But the men would not listen to him. So the man took his concubine and sent her outside to them, and they raped her and abused her throughout the night, and at dawn let her go.

Again, we see a replay and the intense feeling to have ungodly sex.

Jude 1:7 below-shows very clearly, the main reason God destroyed Sodom and Gomorrah and the surrounding towns

"In a similar way, Sodom and Gomorrah and the surrounding towns gave themselves up to sexual immorality and pervasion. They serve as an example of those who suffer the punishment of eternal fire."

Homosexuality is a sin

2 Kings 23:7 - He also tore down the quarters of the male shrine prostitutes that were in the temple of the Lord…

Romans 1:18-27 - The wrath of God is being revealed from heaven against all the godlessness and wickedness of people, who suppress the truth by their wickedness, [19] since what may be known about God is plain to them, because God has made it plain to them. [20] For, since the creation of the world, God's invisible qualities — his eternal power and divine nature — have been clearly seen, being understood from what has been made, so that people are without excuse.

²¹ For although they knew God, they neither glorified him as God nor gave thanks to him, but their thinking became futile and their foolish hearts were darkened. ²² Although they claimed to be wise, they became fools ²³ and exchanged the glory of the immortal God for images made to look like a mortal human being and birds and animals and reptiles.

²⁴ Therefore God gave them over in the sinful desires of their hearts to sexual impurity, for the degrading of their bodies with one another. ²⁵ They exchanged the truth about God for a lie, and worshiped and served created things rather than the Creator, who is forever praised. Amen. Because of this, God gave them over to shameful lusts. Even their women exchanged natural sexual relations for unnatural ones. ²⁷ In the same way the men also abandoned natural relations with women and were inflamed with lust for one another. Men committed shameful acts with other men, and received in themselves the due penalty for their error.

Leviticus 18:22 - Do not have sexual relations with a man as one does with a woman; that is detestable.

Romans 1:26-32 - Because of this, God gave them over to shameful lusts. Even their women exchanged natural sexual relations for unnatural ones. ²⁷ In the same way the men also abandoned natural relations with women and were inflamed with lust for one another. Men committed shameful acts with other men, and received in themselves the due penalty for their error.

²⁸ Furthermore, just as they did not think it worthwhile to retain the knowledge of God, so God gave them over to a depraved mind, so that they do what ought not to be done. ²⁹ They have become filled with every kind of wickedness, evil, greed, and depravity. They are full of envy, murder, strife, deceit, and malice. They are gossips, slanderers, God-haters, insolent, arrogant, and boastful; they invent ways of doing evil; they disobey their parents; ³¹ they have no understanding, no fidelity, no love, no mercy. ³² Although they know God's righteous decree that those who do such things deserve death, they not only continue to do these very things but also approve of those who practice them.

1 Corinthians 6:9-11 - Or do you not know that wrongdoers will not inherit the kingdom of God? Do not be deceived; neither the sexually

immoral nor idolaters nor adulterers nor men who have sex with men [10] nor thieves nor the greedy nor drunkards nor slanderers nor swindlers will inherit the kingdom of God. [11] And that is what some of you were. But you were washed, you were sanctified, you were justified in the name of the Lord Jesus Christ and by the Spirit of our God.

1 Timothy 1:8-10 - We know that the law is good if one uses it properly. [9] We also know that the law is made not for the righteous but for lawbreakers and rebels; the ungodly and sinful; the unholy and irreligious; for those who kill their fathers or mothers; for murderers; [10] for the sexually immoral; for those practicing homosexuality; for slave traders and liars and perjurers; and for whatever else is contrary to the sound doctrine.

Homosexuality is a direct rebellion against God's commands.

Biblically speaking, there is no such thing as gay marriage. God is the Creator and He defines everything.

What about a gay Christian and all the different churches that say it's ok? No such thing according to the Bible and the Creator of all things. Those people especially pastors, will answer to God for teaching lies.

Gay organizations fly a flag that has a rainbow. This is an insult to God, who gave us these beautiful rainbows with a promise to Noah, to never flood the earth again.

A person who has a sinful inclination, orientation, or desire is not justified (by God's standards) in making it right, good, or normal.

The book, "Socialism, The Real History From Plato the Present", quotes the book "Sex and Culture", by J.D Unwin, Anthropologist. After studying 86 different tribes and civilizations over 5,000 years, including Sumerians, Babylonians, Greeks, Romans, Teutons, and Anglo-Saxons, Unwin found that sexual promiscuity [having many sexual partners] always preceded the decline of a civilization.

Sexual immorality

1 Corinthians 5:1-5 - It is actually reported that there is sexual immorality among you, and of a kind that even pagans do not tolerate: A man is sleeping with his father's wife. ²And you are proud! Shouldn't you rather have gone into mourning and have put out of your fellowship the man who has been doing this? ³For my part, even though I am not physically present, I am with you in spirit. As one who is present with you in this way, I have already passed judgment in the name of our Lord Jesus on the one who has been doing this. ⁴So when you are assembled and I am with you in spirit, and the power of our Lord Jesus is present, ⁵hand this man over to Satan for the destruction of the flesh, so that his spirit may be saved on the day of the Lord.

1 Corinthians 6:-9-11 - Or do you not know that wrongdoers will not inherit the kingdom of God? Do not be deceived: <u>Neither the sexually immoral nor idolaters nor adulterers nor men who have sex with men</u> ¹⁰ nor thieves nor the greedy nor drunkards nor slanderers nor swindlers will inherit the kingdom of God. ¹¹And that is what some of you were. But you were washed, you were sanctified, you were justified in the name of the Lord Jesus Christ and by the Spirit of our God.

1 Corinthians 10:8 - We should not commit sexual immorality, as some of them did, and in one day twenty-three thousand of them died.

1 Thessalonians 4:3-7 - It is God's will that you should be sanctified; that you should avoid sexual immorality.

1 Peter 4:1-3 - Therefore, since Christ suffered in his body, arm yourselves also with the same attitude, because whoever suffers in the body is done with sin. ²As a result, they do not live the rest of their earthly lives for evil human desires, but rather for the will of God. ³For you have spent enough time in the past doing what pagans choose to do; living in debauchery, lust, drunkenness, orgies, carousing, and detestable idolatry.

Marriage

God is the definer of marriage and relationships, not man. Marriage is God's institution and man has no right or authority to redefine it; those who do are playing with fire. People who are shacking up and who are not married to each other do not have God's blessings in those relationships. How can God bless a homosexual marriage or an unmarried man and woman living together, who have not followed God's advice?

God is a Holy God and wishes to save all of us, so repent, follow the Bible and get Reborn.

Sex outside of a man's and woman's marriage is a very serious violation of your own body. If you study the Scriptures, you'll see it's more serious than many other sins.

1 Corinthians 6:19-20 - Therefore, since Christ suffered in his body, arm yourselves also with the same attitude, because whoever suffers in the body is done with sin. [2] As a result, they do not live the rest of their earthly lives for evil human desires, but rather for the will of God. [3] For you have spent enough time in the past doing what pagans choose to do, living in debauchery, lust, drunkenness, orgies, carousing, and detestable idolatry.

Transgenderism

In Genesis 6:4, the Nephilim (ne-phi-lim), who the Jewish say are fallen angels, came to earth and had sex with the human women. Their offspring were giants. Some say it would be impossible for a spirit angel to have sex with a human being. However, the Bible says that God does not lie and that the Bible was inspired by Him. Several years ago, man would have said it would be impossible for a man to perfectly pass himself off as a woman. Well, it has happened. Sixty years ago, if you told someone that in the near future Man will be able to visit the moon, they would have laughed at you.

Transgenderism is the newest and grandest expansion into self-rule and rebellion against God.

Sex, sexuality, gender roles, and genders are God's creation and part of His created order.

Public schools and private organizations are allowing "transgender" children and adults to use whichever restroom they want, and allowing boys/men and girls/women to play on the opposite sex sports teams.

Recently boys/men who call themselves female transgender have excelled in sports; one won two Gold Medals for weight lifting, another won the NCAA Division II National Championship in the 400-meter run, and another won Connecticut's state open championship for the 200-meter dash at the high school level.

Many young women who have worked hard for years to excel in their chosen sport are being beaten by transgender girls/women.

Racism

Racism is not a skin problem but a sin problem. Some people believe we are prejudiced since birth and one needs to overcome this temptation.

The Bible thoroughly documents that all people descend from one man - 1 Corinthians 15:45, and one woman - Genesis 3:20; and are of one blood - Acts 17:26 and Malachi 2:10. This means that every person's family tree is traced back to Adam and Eve.

Racism, in any form, rejects the equality assigned by God the Creator.

To say or believe you are better than someone else or they're no good or they're inferior, is to criticize God Himself on the quality of His creations.

— —

What Does the Bible say about Abortion?

1 Timothy 2:15 - But women will be saved through childbearing, if they continue in faith, love, and holiness with propriety.

Jeremiah 1:5 - Before <u>I formed you in the womb, I knew you; before you were born I set you apart</u>; I appointed you as a prophet to the nations.

Psalms 139:13-16 - For you created my inmost being; <u>you knit me together in my mother's womb.</u>[14] I praise you because I am fearfully and wonderfully made; your works are wonderful, I know that full well. [15] My frame was not hidden from you when <u>I was made in the secret place when I was woven together in the depths of the earth.</u>[16] Your eyes saw my unformed body; all the days ordained for me were written in your book before one of them came to be.

Isaiah 49:15 - Can a mother forget the baby at her breast <u>and have no compassion on the child she has borne</u>? Though she may forget, I will not forget you!

Job 31:15 - <u>Did not he who made me in the womb make them</u>? Did not the same one form us both within our mothers?

Psalms 8:5-7 - <u>You have made them a little lower than the angels and crowned them with glory and honor</u> [6] You made them rulers over the works of your hands; you put everything under their feet: [7] all flocks and herds, and the animals of the wild.

Genesis 1:27 - So <u>God created mankind in his own image</u>, in the image of God he created them; male and female he created them.

Proverbs 6:16-19 - There are six things the Lord hates, seven that are detestable to him: haughty eyes a lying tongue, <u>hands that shed innocent blood</u>, a heart that devises wicked schemes, feet that are quick to rush into evil, a false witness who pours out lies, and a person who stirs up conflict in the community.

Isaiah 65:20 - <u>Never again will there be in it an infant who lives but a few days</u>, or an old man who does not live out his years; the one who dies at a hundred will be thought a mere child; the one who fails to reach a hundred will be considered accursed.

Rape

Deuteronomy 22:23-27 - If a man happens to meet in a town a virgin pledged to be married and he sleeps with her, [24] <u>you shall take both of them to the gate of that town and stone them to death</u>; the young woman because she was in a town and did not scream for help, and the man because he violated another man's wife. You must purge the evil from among you.

Deuteronomy 22:25 - But if out in the country a man happens to meet a young woman pledged to be married and rapes her, only <u>the man who has done this shall die.</u>

Before birth

Exodus 21:22-25 - If people are fighting and hit a pregnant woman and she gives birth prematurely, but there is no serious injury, the offender must be fined whatever the woman's husband demands and the court allows. [23] But if there is serious injury, you are to take life for life, [24] eye for an eye, tooth for tooth, hand for hand, foot for foot, [25] burn for burn, wound for wound, bruise for bruise.

Born disabled

Isaiah 45:9-11 - Woe to those who quarrel with their Maker, those who are nothing but potsherds among the potsherds on the ground. Does the clay say to the potter, 'What are you making?' Does your work say, 'The potter has no hands'?

Woe to the one who says to a father, 'What have you begotten?' or to a mother, 'What have you brought to birth?' <u>This is what the Lord says, the Holy One of Israel, and its Maker, concerning things to come; Do you question me about my children, or give me orders about the work of my hands?</u>

Who's responsible for life and death?

Deuteronomy 30:19 - This day I call the heavens and the earth as witnesses against you that I have set before you, life and death, blessings and curses. Now choose life, so that you and your children may live.

Are preborn babies Human Beings?

Galatians 1:15 ...when God, who set me apart from my mother's womb and called me by his grace, was pleased.

Ephesians 1:3-4 - Praise be to the God and Father of our Lord Jesus Christ, who has blessed us in the heavenly realms with every spiritual blessing in Christ. [4] For he chose us in him before the creation of the world to be holy and blameless in his sight.

Luke 1:41-44 - When Elizabeth heard Mary's greeting, the baby leaped in her womb, and Elizabeth was filled with the Holy Spirit. [42] In a loud voice she exclaimed, "Blessed are you among women, and blessed is the child you will bear! [43] But why am I so favored, that the mother of my Lord should come to me? [44] As soon as the sound of your greeting reached my ears, the baby in my womb leaped for joy."

Anyone who says that Abortion, Homosexuality, Transgenderism, and Same-Sex Marriage are okay and acceptable, have no idea on what being a Christian is all about.

If you have a son or daughter that is gay or wants an abortion, besides discouraging them, tell them those types of behaviors are not allowed in your Christian home.

Jesus says in;

Luke 12:51-53 "Do you think I came to bring peace on earth? No, I tell you, but division. [52] From now on there will be five in one family divided against each other, three against two, and two against three. [53] They will be divided; father against son, and son against father; mother against daughter, and daughter against mother; mother-in-law against daughter-in-law, and daughter-in-law against mother-in-law."

Jesus also said in;

Matthew 10:37 - Anyone who loves their father or mother more than me is not worthy of me; anyone who loves their son or daughter more than me is not worthy of me.

Slavery

The Scriptures do not support slavery where you own the person as personal property and can abuse them. The Scriptures discuss bond and servant slavery; where there was a debt owed and specifically had laws on their humane treatment and when they were allowed to be released. Slaves trading in the Bible, where there was abuse and kidnapping was a serious charge and offenders were to be punished by death.

1 Timothy 1:9-10 - We also know that <u>the law is made not for the righteous but for lawbreakers and rebels, the ungodly and sinful, the unholy and irreligious</u>, for those who kill their fathers or mothers, for murderers, [10] for the sexually immoral, for those practicing homosexuality, <u>for slave traders</u> and liars and perjurers, and for whatever else is contrary to the sound doctrine.

Exodus 21:16 - Anyone who kidnaps someone is to be put to death, whether the victim has been sold or is still in the kidnapper's possession.

Astrology, Magic, Mediums, Wizards, Palm or Hand Readers, Tarot Card Readers, and Sorcery

Those involved with these practices are detestable (intense dislike) to God. Christians need to stay far and clear of being involved in these practices because evil spirits are the influencers.

Astrology - following the signs and readings of the month, you were born in.

Magic - exploiting supernatural powers.

Mediums - Someone who communicates with the spirits of the dead.

Wizards - a pretender to supernatural knowledge

Palm, hand readers, and tarot card readers - predict one's character, their behavior, ones past, present, and future (fortune-telling), all of these professions are called deviators in the Bible and will lead a Christian astray.

Sorcery - the use of power from an evil spirit, like using spells and communicating with the evil spirits

Leviticus 19:31 - Do not turn to mediums or seek out spiritists, for <u>you will be defiled by them</u>. I am the Lord your God.

Leviticus 20:6 - <u>I will set my face against anyone who turns to mediums and spiritists to prostitute themselves by</u> following them, and I will cut them off from their people.

1 Samuel 28:7-11 - Saul then said to his attendants, "Find me a woman who is a medium, so I may go and inquire of her." "There is one in Endor," they said.

[8] So Saul disguised himself, putting on other clothes and at night he and two men went to the woman. "Consult a spirit for me," he said, "and bring up for me the one I name."

[9] But the woman said to him, "Surely, you know what Saul has done. He has cut off the mediums and spiritists from the land. Why have you set a trap for my life to bring about my death?" [10] Saul swore to her by the Lord, "As surely as the Lord lives, you will not be punished for this." Then the woman asked, "Whom shall I bring up for you?" "Bring up Samuel," he said. When the woman saw Samuel, she cried out at the top of her voice and said to Saul, "Why have you deceived me? You are Saul!"

[16] Samuel said, "Why do you consult me, now that the Lord has departed from you and become your enemy? [17] The Lord has done what he predicted through me. The Lord has torn the kingdom out of your hands and given it to one of your neighbors—to David. [18] Because you did not obey the Lord or carry out his fierce wrath against the Amalekites, the

Lord has done this to you today. [19] The Lord will deliver both Israel and you into the hands of the Philistines, and tomorrow you and your sons will be with me. The Lord will also give the army of Israel into the hands of the Philistines."

Deuteronomy 18:9-13 - When you enter the land the Lord your God is giving you, do not learn to imitate the detestable ways of the nations there. [10] <u>Let no one be found among you who sacrifices their son or daughter in the fire, who practices divination or sorcery, interprets omens, engages in witchcraft, 11 or casts spells, or who is a medium or spiritist or who consults the dead</u>. [12] Anyone who does these things is detestable to the Lord; because of these same detestable practices, the Lord your God will drive out those nations before you. [13] You must be blameless before the Lord your God.

Exodus 22:18 - <u>Do not allow a sorceress to live.</u>

Reading the astrology in the newspaper;

Isaiah 47:13 - All the counsel you have received has only worn you out! <u>Let your astrologers come forward, those stargazers who make predictions month by month, let them save you from what is coming upon you.</u>

Palm reading, horoscopes, astrology, crystal gazing tarot cards, and Ouija boards;

Leviticus 19:26 - Do not eat any meat with the blood still in it. <u>Do not practice divination or seek omens.</u>

The main problem with above practices is that these professions are communicating with evil spirits. Evil spirits are stationed in localities, and are very familiar with the persons (who is paying for these services and the dead person in question) personality, voice, and habits.

If we had the ability to see with spiritual eyes, we would be able to see these evil spirits around us.

Evolution; the Biggest Lie in America

Evolution is a belief that man was created without the help of a god or a super being. Whatever a person believes in becomes a statement that something is true and/or exists. <u>Evolution is a religion</u>.

Evolutionists believe that the characteristics of a species change over the years; all species are related and gradually change over time, relying on the process of natural selection. Natural selection is the process by which organisms adapt and change.

Evolutionists believe that man evolved millions of years ago, out of nothing. Evolution says there is no God; you enjoy life, live once and die. Christians believe that God created man and animals according to its own kind, almost six thousand years ago.

The Bible teaches us in;

Genesis 1:1-27 - In the beginning **God created the heavens and the earth.** [3] And God said, "Let there be light," and there was light. [4] God saw that the light was good, and he separated the light from the darkness. [5] **God called the light "day," and the darkness he called "night."** And God said, "Let there be a vault between the waters to separate water from water." [7] So God made the vault and separated the water under the vault from the water above it. And it was so. [8] **God called the vault "sky."**

[9] And God said, "Let the water under the sky be gathered to one place, **and let dry ground appear." And it was so.** [10] **God called the dry ground "land,"** and the gathered waters he called "seas." [11] **Then God said, "Let the land produce vegetation: seed-bearing plants and trees on the land that bear fruit with seed in it, according to their various kinds.** And it was so. [12] The land produced vegetation: plants bearing seed according to their kinds and trees bearing fruit with seed in it according to their kinds.

¹⁴ And God said, "Let there be lights in the vault of the sky to separate the day from the night, and let them serve as signs to mark sacred times, and days and years, ¹⁵ and let them be lights in the vault of the sky to give light on the earth." And it was so. ¹⁶ God made two great lights—the greater light to govern the day and the lesser light to govern the night. He also made the stars. ¹⁷ God set them in the vault of the sky to give light on the earth, ¹⁸ to govern the day and the night, and to separate light from the darkness.

²⁰ And God said, "Let the water teem with living creatures, and let birds fly above the earth across the vault of the sky." ²¹ So God created the great creatures of the sea and every living thing with which the water teems and that moves about in it, **according to their kinds**, and every winged bird according to its kind. And God saw that it was good. ²² God blessed them and said, "Be fruitful and increase in number and fill the water in the seas, and let the birds increase on the earth."

²⁴ And God said, "Let the land produce living creatures according to their kinds: the livestock, the creatures that move along the ground, and the wild animals, each according to its kind." And it was so. ²⁵ **God made the wild animals according to their kinds, the livestock according to their kinds, and all the creatures that move along the ground according to their kinds.** And God saw that it was good. ²⁶ Then God said, "**Let us make mankind in our image, in our likeness**, so that they may rule over the fish in the sea and the birds in the sky, over the livestock and all the wild animals, and overall the creatures that move along the ground." ²⁷ So, God created mankind in his own image, in the image of **God he created them; male and female he created them.**

Christianity and Evolution only have one thing in common; they're both beliefs and religions (they both make a commitment or devotion to their beliefs).

Definition of Science

The definition of Science is that true knowledge derives from Observation, Study, and the Testing of Evidence.

Science requires observation and study over time, to measure changes. Since man never studied; the creation of the heavens, the earth, and man, since the beginning of time, they have not observed these so-called changes. So according to true science, if it's not observable and testable, it is not Science. Has man identified any changes in the species of man or animal in the last 200 years? No.

Macro and Micro adaptation

Macroevolution is where a dog produces a non-dog or some type of another animal. This has never happened. <u>Nor has the millions of fossil evidence ever shown this to happen.</u>

Micro adaptation is when a dog produces a dog, or where a human produces its own kind.

Genesis 1:24 And God said, "Let the land produce <u>living creatures according to their kinds."</u>

Evolutionists cannot provide one thread of evidence that macroevolution is possible.

Evolution goes from less complex forms of life to more complex; like bacteria becoming a fish, which became amphibians (frogs), and then lizards, mammals, and then humans. Evolution says you came from nothing, then from an animal to a human being.

Natural Selection is the process according to Evolution, through which, populations of living organisms adapt and change - National Geographic.

Survival of the Fittest is the natural process, according to Evolution where organism's best adjust to their environment and are the most successful in surviving.

This theory of survival of the fittest; where only the best survive, is a very selfish theory. Christians help others to survive by providing food, shelter, medicine, and the Truth.

Fossil record

The fossil record over the years does not show transitional forms, <u>the stages where one type of creature evolved into another</u>. On the earth, there should be millions and millions of transitional evidence, yet, to date there is none.

Schools

In public schools and Catholic schools, Evolutionary theory is taught and is the biggest lie in the United States, because it violates physics and what God has taught us in the Bible. If your Christian children go to one of these schools, they only offer an opportunity to confuse your children.

Since Creationism is not allowed in public schools, Evolution should not be allowed, since both are religions.

Comments from noted Scientists

Albert Einstein was widely acknowledged as one of the greatest physicists of all time, said, "I don't believe the theory of evolution; I think we were all specially created."

Isaac Newton, Mathematician, Physicist, Astronomer, Alchemist, Theologian, and Author, said, "The most beautiful system of the sun, planets, and cosmos could only proceed from the counsel and dominion of an intelligent and powerful Being."

Louis Pasteur, Chemist, and Microbiologist, said, "The more I study nature, the more I am amazed at the Creator."

Lee Spetner, Ph.D. Physics said, "On experimental grounds, I have shown that there are no known random mutations that have added any genetic information to the organism. <u>I go through a list of the best examples of mutations offered by Evolutionists and show that each of them loses generic information rather than gains it."</u>

More Scriptures that say Man was created by God and that evolution is a fairy tale;

Romans 1:19-20 - since what may be known about God is plain to them, because God has made it plain to them. [20] For since the creation of the world, God's invisible qualities — **his eternal power and divine nature — have been clearly seen, being understood from what has been made, so that people are without excuse.**

Romans 1:25 - They exchanged the truth about God for a lie, **and worshiped and served created things rather than the Creator**, who is forever praised. Amen.

John 1:1-3 - In the beginning was the Word, and the Word was with God, and the Word was God. [2] He was with God in the beginning. [3] **Through him all things were made; without him, nothing was made that has been made.**

Hebrews 11:**3 - By faith we understand that the universe was formed at God's command**, so that what is seen was not made out of what was visible.

1 Thessalonians 5:21 - "Test everything. Hold on to the good."

1 Tim.6: 20-21 - "Turn away from Godless chatter and the opposing ideas of what is falsely called knowledge."

Closing

No matter what sins one has committed; murder, abortion, homosexuality, incest, etc., God is willing to forgive you if you repent, follow Jesus and get Born Again.

Ezekiel 33:11 - **Say to them, "As surely as I live," declares the Sovereign Lord, "I take no pleasure in the death of the wicked, but rather that they turn from their ways and live. Turn! Turn from your evil ways! Why will you die, people of Israel?"**

The fact that Jesus purchased a plan of salvation for us **is the greatest news the world has ever received.**

Examine yourself-are you following the True God?

Deuteronomy 13:1 If a prophet, or one who foretells by dreams, appears among you and announces to you a sign or wonder, [2] and if the sign or wonder spoken of, takes place, and the prophet says, "Let us follow other gods" (gods you have not known) "and let us worship them," [3] you must not listen to the words of that prophet or dreamer. The Lord your God is testing you to find out whether you love him with all your heart and with all your soul.

2 John 1:10-11 If anyone comes to you and does not bring this teaching, do not take them into your house or welcome them. [11] Anyone who welcomes them shares in their wicked work.

2 Corinthians 11:13 For such people are false apostles, deceitful workers, masquerading as apostles of Christ.

2 Corinthians 13:5 Examine yourselves to see whether you are in the faith; test yourselves. Do you not realize that Christ Jesus is in you, unless, of course, you fail the test?

Acts 17:11 – Now, the Berean Jews were of more noble character than those in Thessalonica, for they received the message with great eagerness and examined the Scriptures every day to see if what Paul said was true.

1 Thessalonians 5:21 – But test them all; hold on to what is good.

2 Thessalonians 2:15 - So then, brothers and sisters, stand firm and hold fast to the teachings we passed on to you, whether by word of mouth or by letter.

Romans 12:2 - Do not conform to the pattern of this world, but be transformed by the renewing of your mind. <u>Then you will be able to test and approve what God's will is—his good, pleasing, and perfect will.</u>

Romans 16:17-18 - I urge you, brothers and sisters, to watch out for those who cause divisions and put obstacles in your way that are contrary to the teaching you have learned. Keep away from them. [18] For such people are not serving our Lord Christ, but their own appetites. <u>By smooth talk and flattery, they deceive the minds of naive people.</u>

Matthew 7:15-16 - Watch out for false prophets. <u>They come to you in sheep's clothing, but inwardly they are ferocious wolves.</u> [16] By their fruit you will recognize them.

Matthew 24:4-5 - Jesus answered, "Watch out that no one deceives you. [5] For <u>many will come in my name</u>, claiming, 'I am the Messiah,' and will deceive many."

Colossians 2:8 - See to it that no one takes you captive through hollow and deceptive philosophy, **which depends on human tradition** and the elemental spiritual forces of this world rather than on Christ.

1 Timothy 4:1-2 - The Spirit clearly says that in later times some will abandon the faith and follow deceiving spirits and things taught by demons. [2] Such teachings come through hypocritical liars, whose consciences have been seared as with a hot iron.

1 Timothy 6:3-4 - If anyone teaches otherwise and does not agree to the sound instruction of our Lord Jesus Christ and to godly teaching, [4] they are conceited and understand nothing.

Ephesians 5:6 - Let no one deceive you with empty words, for because of such things God's wrath comes on those who are disobedient.

1 John 4:2-6 - <u>This is how you can recognize the Spirit of God:</u> Every spirit that acknowledges that Jesus Christ has come in the flesh is from God, [3] but every spirit that does not acknowledge Jesus is not from God. This is the spirit of the antichrist, which you have heard is coming and even now is already in the world.

2 Peter 2:5-8 - For this very reason, make every effort to add to your faith goodness; and to goodness, knowledge; [6] and to knowledge, self-control; and to self-control, perseverance; and to perseverance, godliness; [7] and to godliness, mutual affection; and to mutual affection, love. [8] For if you possess these qualities in increasing measure, they will keep you from being ineffective and unproductive in your knowledge of our Lord Jesus Christ.

Eternal life

1 Corinthians 15:55 "Where, O death, is your victory? Where, O death is your sting?

1 John 5:11 - And this is the testimony: God has given us eternal life, and this life is in His Son

The Apostle Paul says, in 1 Corinthians 9:24, "…Run in such a way as to get the prize." And in verse 25, "…we do it to get a crown that will last forever."

Be Smart! Concentrate all your efforts on where you're going to be for Eternity; before concerning yourself in finishing school, trying to perfect your athletic skills, working in a job, paying your monthly mortgage on a house or rent, raising children, worrying about your health and retiring.

When all is said and done, the majority of the human race will not inherit Everlasting Life. Be smart, be one who wants to live forever with God and Jesus

Matthew 7:13-14 - Enter through the narrow gate. <u>For wide is the gate and broad is the road that leads to destruction, and many enter through it</u>. [14] But small is the gate and narrow the road that leads to life and only a few find it.

Matthew 7:21-23 - Not everyone who says to me, 'Lord, Lord,' will enter the kingdom of heaven, <u>but only the one who does the will of my Father who is in heaven</u>. [22] Many will say to me on that day, 'Lord, Lord, did we not prophesy in your name and in your name drive out demons and in your name perform many miracles?' [23] Then I will tell them plainly, I never knew you. Away from me, you evildoers!

Luke 13:24-25 - Make every effort to enter through the narrow door, because many, I tell you, will try to enter and will not be able to. Once the owner of the house gets up and closes the door, you will stand outside knocking and pleading, 'Sir, open the door for us.' "But he will answer, 'I don't know you or where you come from.'

Matthew 19:24 - Again I tell you, it is easier for a camel to go through the eye of a needle than for someone who is rich to enter the kingdom of God.

John 10:9 - I am the gate; whoever enters through me will be saved. They will come in and go out and find pasture.

Isaiah 35:8 - And a highway will be there; it will be called the Way of Holiness; it will be for those who walk on that Way. The unclean will not journey on it; wicked fools will not go about on it.

John 14:6 - Jesus answered, "I am the way and the truth and the life. **No one comes to the Father except through me."**

John 1:12 - Yet to all who did receive him, to those who believed in his name, **he gave the right to become children of God.**

BIBLIOGRAPHY SOURCES

Questions about the Holy Spirit, S. Michael Houdmann

GotQuestions.org

The Code of the Holy Spirit, Perry Stone, 2013

Fast Facts on False Teachings, Ron Carson and Ed Decker, 1994

The Holy Spirit, Perry Stone

Heaven, Randy Alcorn, 2004

50 Years in the "Church" of Rome, Charles Chiniquy

Answers to my Catholic Friends, Thomas Heinze

The Two Babylon's, Alexander Hislop

Understanding Roman Catholicism, by Rick Jones

The History of Tithing's, Jayson D. Bradley

Preparing For Eternity, Mike Gendron, 2011

What Does The Bible Teach About Self-Defense? Can A Christian use A Gun In Self-Defense? David L. Brown, Ph.D.

Quick Answers to Social Issues, Bryan Osborne, 2019

Evolution vs. Creation, Russ Miller

Socialism, the Real History From Plato to The Present-How the Deep State Capitalizes on Crises to Consolidate Control, William J. Federer, 2021

ABOUT THE AUTHOR

Gregg Gonzales was born and lives in Santa Fe, New Mexico. For the first thirty years of his life, Gregg was a Catholic and attended mostly Catholic schools from grades 1st. through 12th. For the second thirty-four years of his life, he has attended Bible churches. Gregg has been part of the ministry at the State Penitentiary of New Mexico's Maximum Security and teaches Bible Classes.

Gregg is the author of;

- The First Pioneers of the Uppermost Pecos, 2014

- The First Archibeque's, Larranaga's and Tapia's to settle New Mexico, 2014

- The Spanish Occupation of New Mexico - Was it Worth it? 2015

- The First Hispanos to Settle Pecos and the Pecos Pueblo, 2017

- Follow the True God of the Bible for Everlasting Life, 2022

Gregg can be reached at gggggonzales@gmail.com.

THE LITTLEST FIREFIGHTER CALLED BOBSY

In Phoenix, Arizona; a 26-year-old mother stared down at her son who was dying of terminal leukemia.

Although her heart was filled with sadness, she also had a strong feeling of determination. Like any parent, she wanted her son to grow up and fulfill all his dreams. Now, that was no longer possible. Leukemia would see to that. But she still wanted her son's dreams to come true. She took her son's hand and asked, "Bopsy", did you ever think about what you wanted to be once you grew up?

Did you ever dream and wish what you would do with your life?" Mommy, "I always wanted to be a fireman when I grew up." Mom smiled back and said, "Let's see if we can make your wish come true."

Later that day she went to her local fire department in Phoenix, Arizona, where she met Fireman Bob, who had a heart as big as Phoenix. She explained her son's final wish and asked if it might be possible to give her six-year-old son a ride around the block on a fire engine.

Fireman Bob said, "Look, we can do better than that. If you'll have your son ready at seven o'clock Wednesday morning, we'll make him an honorary fireman for the whole day. He can come down to the fire station, eat with us, go out on all the fire calls the whole nine yards! And if you'll give us his sizes, we'll get a real fire uniform for him; with a chiefs hat-not a toy one-with the emblem of the Phoenix Fire Department on it, a yellow slicker like we wear and rubber boots. They're all manufactured right here in Phoenix, so we can get them fast."

Three days later Fireman Bob picked up Bopsy, dressed him in his fire uniform and escorted him from his hospital bed to the waiting hook and ladder truck. Bopsy got to sit on the back of the truck and helped steer it back to the fire station.

He was in heaven. There were three fire calls in Phoenix that day and Bopsy got to go out on all three calls. He rode in the different fire engines, the paramedic's van, and even the fire chief's car. He was also videotaped for the local news program.

All of Bopsy's dreams came true, and with all the love and attention that was lavished upon him, so deeply touched Bopsy that he lived three months longer than any doctor thought possible.

One night all of his vital signs began to drop dramatically and the head nurse, who believed in the hospice concept that no one should die alone, began to call the family members to the hospital.

Then she remembered the day Bopsy had spent as a fireman, so she called the Fire Chief and asked if it would be possible to send a fireman in uniform to the hospital to be with Bopsy as he made his transition. The chief replied, "We can do better than that. We'll be there in five minutes. Will you please do me a favor? When you hear the sirens screaming and see the lights flashing, will you announce over the PA system that there is not a fire?

It's just the fire department coming to see one of its finest members one more time. And will you open the window to his room?"

About five minutes later a hook and ladder truck arrived at the hospital and extended its ladder up to Bopsy's third-floor open window.

Sixteen firefighters climbed up the ladder into Bopsy's room. With his mother's permission, they hugged him and held him and told him how much they loved him.

With his dying breath, Bopsy looked up at the fire chief and said, "Chief am I really a fireman now?"

"Bopsy, you are, and the Head Chief, Jesus, is holding your hand," the chief said. With those words, Bopsy smiled and said, "I know, He's been holding my hand all day, and the angels have been singing." He closed his eyes one last time.

"Bopsy" is actually 7-year-old Frank Salazar (his family called him "Bopsy") and he was the first child to be helped by the Make-A-Wish Foundation, an organization that fulfills the wishes of children with life-threatening illnesses. This story is from 1981 and part of one of three wishes that Bopsy had. The other two were to visit Disneyland and ride in a hot-air balloon. All his wishes were fulfilled.

FOR NOTES

FOR NOTES

www.ingramcontent.com/pod-product-compliance
Lightning Source LLC
Chambersburg PA
CBHW051519120626
46551CB00012B/992